HOW TO SPEAK WITHOUT FEAR

HOW TO SPEAK WITHOUT FEAR

NATALIE ROGERS

Ward Lock Limited · London

First published in United States of America in 1982 by Dodd, Mead & Company, New York.

This edition first published in Great Britain in 1984 by Ward Lock Limited, 82 Gower Street, London WC1E 6EQ, a Pentos Company.

Printed and bound in Great Britain

British Library Cataloguing in Publication Data

Rogers, Natalie
How to speak without fear.
1. Public speaking
I. Title
808.5'1 PN4121

ISBN 0-7063-6301-9

To the memory of my mother,
Rose Kessler Rogers.
Her sense of hope is my dearest legacy.

Contents

	Acknowledgments	ix
	Introduction	1
1.	Why You Are Afraid	7
2.	Controlling Your Fear Response	30
3.	How to Begin Talking	43
4.	The Talk-Power Action Formula (The Building-Block Approach)	70
5.	How to Begin to Write a Speech (The Introductory Section)	80
6.	Getting Your Message Across (The Topic and Thesis Sentence)	91
7.	How to Get People to Care (The Background Section)	108
8.	How to Think Systematically (The Point Section)	121
9.	How to Say Goodbye (The Conclusion)	141
10.	How to Use Visual Aids	156
11.	Taking Questions from the Floor	168
12.	The Public Speaker's Bill of Rights	183
13.	Schedules for Busy People	193

14. Making the Transition from Living Room to the Public Arena 203

Appendixes

1. Panic Clinic for Public Speaking 214
2. Advanced Sense-Memory Imaging Rehearsal 221
3. The Kinesthetic Rehearsal 225
4. Participation in Meetings and Classrooms 228
5. Video as a Training Tool 234
6. Stuttering 236

Index 238

Acknowledgments

This book was born when my husband, Harold Herbstman, urged me to try to translate the work that I was doing in my seminars into a book. For his belief that this could be done, and for all of the good "vibes" that he sent out about this project from beginning to end, I would like to say that I am deeply grateful.

For the monumental task of editing and helping me to stay on target, I must say thank you to the very gifted John Malone. To Judy Davanzo, who has got to be one of the most patient, loyal, and generous people I know, I wish to acknowledge the enormous role she played in this book by typing, keeping things in impeccable order, and being there when she was needed.

I owe an eternal debt of gratitude to my dear friend and agent, Anne Borchardt, for the intelligence of her advice, her support, and the very special concern that she had for my manuscript. I am also indebted to Herbert Fensterheim, Ph.D., Clinical Associate Professor of Psychology in Psychiatry, Cornell University Medical College, and Head, Behavior Therapy Treatment and Study, Payne Whitney Clinic, the New York Hospital, for the impact of his remarkable mind upon the development of my thinking. To my students from the National Congress of Neighborhood Women as well as Baruch College, Bernice Amalfitano, Sally Touma, Mary Lococero, John McLaughlin, Diane Kent, Dr. Lisa Wasserman, and Elizabeth Kaufman, thank you for the excerpts of your work that I was able to use. Thank you also Warren B. Sheridan of J.C. Penney. I would also like to say special words of thanks to Shelly Garnet and Mrs. Bernard P. Borchardt, who first invited me to introduce the Talk-Power program at the 92nd St. YM-YWHA, to professor Arlene Julius, who invited me to bring my Panic Clinic to Baruch College. Thank you also to Marci Goldstein, Ph.D, Director of Training of the American Woman's Economic Development Corporation, who encouraged and supported the growth of this program when she was the Director of Adult Education at Baruch College. I would like to extend a very special thank you to Joan Grad at J.C. Penney National Headquarters in New York, who invited me to bring the Talk-Power program to this corporation, where the continuous running of the ten-week seminars over a four-year period provided the continuity necessary for the growth of this program. To my dear friends and colleagues Terry Haywood, Merle Kroop, M.D., John Chapman, and Helene Sands, thank you for your suggestions and encouragement. Thank you also for your support and enthusiasm to my sisters, Gail Katz and Beverly Rogers, and of course to my original role model, my aunt, Frances Kessler.

To Max and Hilda Wolkowitz my eternal gratitude for the many hours of tender loving care that you gave to my daughter, Colette, so that I was able to go to my work with peace of mind.

To my editor at Dodd Mead, Margaret Norton, a sincere note of thanks for the care and concern that you gave to my manuscript.

This acknowledgment would not be complete without the expression of gratitude that I feel to the many many hundreds of students, clients, and patients who form a part of the living laboratory where these ideas and techniques were nurtured and developed.

Finally, to my beautiful daughter, Colette, thank you for the space you made in your life for me and my work.

"The brain is unlike any organ in the body in that its internal structure is always changing and developing as a result of experience. This gives it the unlimited capacity for learning."

—Peter Russell
The Brain Book

Introduction

Ten years ago, when I was embarking on my second career as a psychotherapist after having spent many years in the theater, I took a course in oral communication.

I would sit in class listening to lengthy speeches being delivered, watching the nervously uncomfortable students make their presentations, and it seemed to me there was no visible improvement in their performance over time. The speeches were just as ineffectual at the end of the semester as they had been at the beginning. The students looked just as uncomfortable as they had on the very first day.

As a theater person with years of acting, teaching, and directing experience under my belt, I sat there in utter disbelief. How, I asked, could the instructor not be aware of the jerks, tics, and total state of terror that most of these unfortunates were so obviously experiencing? How could she fail to address one word to this issue? How could she continue to discuss the principles of persuasive speech when it was absolutely impossible to make logical sense out of most of the speeches being presented? How could the disembodied principles of oral communication ever relate to the spectrum of pain so evident in that classroom? These students, most of whom had never in their lives been asked to stand up and give even the simplest of directions to a group, were now tackling complete writing and speaking assignments from day one.

When I recovered from the sheer amazement of it all, I had what you might call a moment of "aha." That is, I had a wonderful idea. I realized that the training that proved helpful to actors in overcoming their inhibitions could be applied to public speaking. With this in mind, I designed a step-by-step plan for acquiring the basic presentational skills.

That idea has been developed over the past ten years into a systematic training program enhanced by my experience as a behavioral psychotherapist. The knowledge and training that I have accumulated over this period have expanded the scope and dimension of the program I developed by setting it in a theoretical framework that is both scientific and practical.

I first taught this program, which I called Talk-Power, at the 92nd Street YM/YWHA in New York City. I went on to conduct seminars and courses at LaGuardia Community College, Baruch College, the National Congress for Neighborhood Women, and for such corporations as J.C. Penney and IBM. I have also had many individual clients, including not only lawyers and business executives, but also a number of political figures. My experience in dealing with their problems has helped me to perfect a program that has literally changed the lives of hundreds of my students and clients.

The purpose of this book is to share this idea with you so that you too can have Talk-Power.

WHY IS TALK-POWER DIFFERENT?

Talk-Power is different from all other methods of teaching public speaking because it is the only program that deals with fear as the basic problem standing between you and successful public speaking. The Talk-Power program utilizes a synthesis of techniques derived from three different fields—behavior modification, acting technique, and speech crafting—in order gradually to change your fear response to a controlled response.

In the traditional approach, fear of public speaking is dismissed as an isolated occurrence, a simple case of nervousness that can be dealt with through a series of hints, tips, advice, and gimmicks. The traditional assumption has been that willpower can do it for you. If you just think positively, you can will your heart to stop beating too fast when you have to speak in public.

You probably have already discovered for yourself that this approach does not work. As many studies show conclusively, the fear response is so powerful and automatic that willpower is ineffectual in relieving it.

In the Talk-Power system the significance of the fear response is fully acknowledged and approached scientifically from a behavioral point of view. This means that *although you have learned to respond to the problem of speaking in public with fear, you can now, through planned and organized training, learn a new and more satisfying way to take control of yourself when you have to speak in public.* The problem of the fear response is thoroughly and systematically worked out through use of a unique series of sequential exercises derived from the acting and the behavioral repertoires. Designed to slow down your internal response system and deepen your concentration, these exercises are very simple to do, and yet they end the knee-jerk panic that so often accompanies speaking in public.

Another area where the Talk-Power system differs from other approaches to public speaking is in the detailed and systematic attention it pays to actual crafting of the speech. By contrast, according to traditional methods, students are assigned complete speeches from the very first day. Even if that speech is only three or four minutes long, a student who has no knowledge of the basic structural rules for organizing an oral presentation will never be able to master the task or develop a repeatable technique for doing so. It is like the golfer who never learns to perfect his swing because he is rushed into competitive games with emphasis upon the score before fundamental attention is given to proper swing technique.

THE BUILDING-BLOCK APPROACH

The Talk-Power program teaches the craft of speech writing through the use of a simple formula. This formula breaks every speech into seven basic sections. Each section is worked on individually. Initially the sections are never longer than one minute of speaking time. After each section is completed, an assignment is included for a complete rehearsal. In this way you begin your training with very small units that grow longer as you complete more sections of your speech. In addition you learn how to group and categorize your ideas around one central thesis, thereby becoming familiar with the process of systematic thinking.

Organizing a speech in this manner reinforces your confidence, because the structure of the formula guides and directs you so specifically that it is impossible to feel overwhelmed or lost. In addition, the rules for designing a balanced, well put-together talk are easily learned and remembered.

This building-block approach for breaking a speech down into a series of small steps is unique to this program and has proven successful in two crucial areas. First, through a gradual series of steps, it desensitizes the fearful speaker to the fear of public speaking. Second, it gives one mastery in speech-writing skills. This two-pronged approach puts a minimum of pressure upon the student, since it conditions his or her body to respond in new and more desirable ways to the stress of speaking at the same time that it helps overcome fear of writing and delivering a talk. (For truly phobic individuals, the Panic Clinic for Public Speaking, Appendix 1, offers a more basic set of exercises to prepare them for entry into the Talk-Power program.)

Because this program deals with the issue of fear of public speaking as a perfectly natural and universal condition, the system of training makes it possible for feelings of control to develop very early on in training. These feelings of control give hope and encouragement and are crucial to the reversal of the fear response. As you follow the systematic practice schedules that are laid out step by step, feelings of control will grow into a sense of mastery, eventually eliminating the terror that comes with the thought of having to speak in public. This is the secret of the program and why it has succeeded where conventional methods have failed.

As Joanne R. remarked the night before she was to give her first four-minute presentation to a group of fifty at her company, "I am nervous, but I know I can do it because I am no longer afraid."

The Talk-Power approach has been extraordinarily successful in helping people to overcome their fear of public speaking and in turning out speakers who look and sound professional. For that reason this book has been organized to duplicate the structure of actual training seminars. To that end, each chapter contains a sequential aspect or step of the program's formula plus instructions for the writing and rehearsal of that step. As you follow the assignments outlined in each chapter, you will find that a gradual desensitization process begins to shape and change your fear response into Talk-Power.

CHAPTER 1

Why You Are Afraid

Seated in a semicircle facing a speaker's podium were twelve well-dressed, highly successful men and women. Each held a position of broad responsibility in a large corporation. Yet all of them were attending a Talk-Power seminar because they had encountered serious problems whenever they were required to speak before groups of people. In ordinary conversation they were articulate and at ease, but when faced with the prospect of addressing a group, they invariably went to pieces.

As they discussed their reasons for attending the seminar, there was initially much hesitation and numerous embarrassed silences. But gradually they began to share their stories, stories of the pain and humiliation they had suffered when speaking before groups.

Mr. J., a senior project manager, threw up his hands. "I don't know what happens to me," he said. "I just go into a state of shock when I have to address a group. Last year I was supposed to make an honorary presentation at a dinner, and I had to bow out at the last minute. My knees were shaking so badly I couldn't walk. I can't tell you how embarrassing it was."

"All I had to do was give these guys a short tour of the

department," Bob T., a sales promotion manager, admitted. "But all of a sudden my heart started beating so fast I lost control. Boy, did I mess up. Of course my boss heard about what happened, and that was the end of my move up to advertising manager. It hasn't gotten any better. Even sitting here now, I feel as though my heart was going to jump right out of my chest."

Ms. C. was a marketing publications illustrator who had been with her company for nine years. She told of attending a conference where she found herself unable to talk. "I had a terrific idea, and I was dying to speak up —but I couldn't. It was ridiculous, because I knew most of the people there. But I kept quiet. Then someone else made the exact same suggestion that I had in mind, and everybody said it was brilliant. I could have just kicked myself for missing a great chance to show my boss what I could do."

As a behavioral therapist specializing in public speaking, I have listened to hundreds of similar stories over the past several years. (*The Book of Lists* states that fear of public speaking is the number-one phobia in the United States, affecting a majority of all people. That adds up to literally millions.) Many people come to the Talk-Power seminars filled with despair. They fear that their problems are insurmountable, that they do not have whatever it takes to be able to present in front of other people. Part of the difficulty is that those who are terrified of speaking in public often believe that others who are good at it— politicians, members of the clergy, teachers, etc.—come by their ability naturally, without real effort. Though it is true that occasionally we find an individual who has a natural gift for public speaking, much more often a great deal of hard work and practice has gone into learning how to control feelings, to combat physical discomfort, and to present to an audience convincingly.

Although the ability to speak well before groups may be absolutely essential in some professions, the need to do so can arise in almost any line of work at one time or another, especially if one wishes to move upward in one's profession. The inability to speak before groups can not only be embarrassing, it can cost you a promotion or spoil a chance to demonstrate your expertise at your job.

If you are afraid to speak up before a group or "make a mess of it" when you do speak, you are undermining your own success. The scientific system I have devised is designed to train you systematically to overcome the fears that prevent you, like so many other people, from making the most of your abilities. These are the fears that cause you to stumble over words, repeat yourself, forget important points, or come to a dead halt with no idea what to say next.

SYMPTOMS OF DISTRESS

There are three main categories of symptoms reported by people who have difficulty speaking before groups. First there are the *physical symptoms* of distress. These may begin days before making an actual presentation and show up in the form of a nervous stomach or sleepless nights. During the speech itself, symptoms of physical distress may vary from person to person, but can include any or all of the following:

- Rapid heartbeat
- Trembling knees, making it difficult to get up and

walk to the podium or stand at ease in front of a group
- Quivering voice, often accompanied by a tightness in the throat or an accumulation of phlegm
- Hot flashes or a feeling of faintness
- Stomach nervousness, sometimes to the point of nausea
- Hyperventilation, involving an uncontrolled gasping for air
- Eye tearing or a runny nose

The second category of symptoms affects the *mental processes* during the giving of a speech or talk. Such symptoms may include:

- Repetition of words, phrases, or messages to a degree that makes the speaker sound like a stuck record
- Loss of memory, including the inability to recall facts and figures accurately and the leaving out of important points altogether
- General disorganization
- Thought blockage, causing the speaker to stop dead, having no idea what he or she intended to say next

Physical or mental symptoms of distress are likely to be accompanied or preceded by a variety of *emotional reactions:*

- Feelings of terror, which often arise even before beginning to speak
- A sense of being overwhelmed
- A sense of having lost control of oneself
- Helplessness, a childlike feeling of being unable to cope

- Embarrassment
- Panic
- Feelings of shame and humiliation following a presentation

These three categories of symptoms interact with another. An initial feeling of terror as you sit waiting to be introduced can cause your heart to race uncontrollably. Your pounding heart can make you even more nervous, and your throat may begin to tighten. Physical symptoms can disrupt your mental concentration, causing you to lose track of the organization of your speech. As you stumble over your words, repeat phrases, or leave out ideas, feelings of embarrassment and a loss of control may easily result.

Brief physical symptoms of anxiety can afflict even the most accomplished public speaker; even the most organized of speakers may suffer a mental lapse. But the accomplished and experienced speaker knows how to bring himself back under control, knows how to overcome nervousness or cover up a lapse of thought. The training program I have developed is designed to enable you to do the same.

WHY YOU ARE SO ANXIOUS

Before you can begin to overcome a problem, you must fully understand why the problem exists, what its roots are. Why are you so anxious when you speak before a group of people? The clients and students I have worked with over the years have almost invariably been completely mystified as to why they encounter problems when speaking to groups. "After all," they will say, "I know how to talk."

"My friends tell me I'm very witty, but put me in front of half a dozen people and I'm not just tongue-tied, I'm speechless."

"I spent days preparing for that speech, but as soon as I stood up everything just flew out of my head. I can't understand why!"

Why indeed?

After all, the group you are speaking to may consist of only three or four people. You may even know some of them. Why should you be nervous? What is it that transforms a normally poised and articulate person into a quivering mass of jelly in front of a group?

Whenever you face a group, whether you are sitting or standing, you become *separate from the people you are addressing.* They are listening to you and looking at you. They are together as a group, but you, facing them, are alone.

They have the anonymity of a group, while you have the high visibility of one standing apart. You are, as many of my clients have put it, "on trial." It will seem to you, although not to the audience, that every movement you make, every gesture, every slip of the tongue, is magnified a hundred times in size and importance. It is no wonder that so many people who speak in public feel vulnerable, even threatened. You are making yourself visible to others in a highly exposed way, opening yourself to their microscopic scrutiny. You can't hide. It is not surprising that you may feel terrified, and if your boss or someone else you want to impress is sitting out there looking at you, you have all the more reason to feel like a duck in a shooting gallery.

The fact that you are a good conversationalist doesn't mean anything now. You're not involved in a conversation, and you can no longer draw on your social instincts. You must instead develop *presentational* techniques suited to this new role. You must learn how to shift from your normal *social self* to a *presentational self.* And that is precisely what this training program is designed to help you do.

SPEAKING IN PUBLIC VERSUS HAVING A CONVERSATION

There is a profound difference between social conversation and a formal presentation. In order to be able to make a successful presentation, a significant shift of attention must occur within your consciousness. This shift of attention is essential in order for you to cope with the change taking place as you assume your new role as the leader of the group you are addressing.

Most people have not been trained to make this shift. Unfortunately, most of us are much better prepared to deal with the personal arena than we are with the public. Our social self is well-developed; our presentational self is not.

We are all born into a society in which conversation is a matter of daily exercise. We learn to talk, to listen, to interact, and when to react or not react to others as a matter of familiar experience. We learn to expect the obvious and to interpret more subtle cues. We develop the ability to gauge the feedback we are getting—whether the responses are positive or negative—becoming aware of a system in which smiles, nods, frowns, questions, responses, and interruptions all have their place. We learn to converse with others in a close exchange.

In the context of this familiar conversational experience we feel safe communicating our thoughts. But it is the rare person, the exception, who has been prepared or groomed in any way for the presentational experience, the experience of standing alone at a distance, singled out, talking to a group as a whole.

In a conversational role—whether you are a peer talking to a peer, a friend talking to a friend, a wife talking to a husband, a staff member talking to a superior, a buyer talking to a seller—you know the rules. According to the situation you are in and with whom you are talking, you may be authoritative or deferential, sympathetic or antagonistic, soothing or provocative. But because you are talking *with* someone who is giving you constant feedback, you can adjust your reactions as you go along. The conversational role is by its very nature reciprocal, and you are used to it. Psycholinguist Breyne Arlene Moskowitz believes "that children first learn to develop their language skills through the process of dialogue."

The presentational role, however, implies a totally different set of relationships. To begin with, the give and take of dialogue so integral to social conversation becomes a process of monologue. In addition, **the moment you begin speaking to a group you automatically become the *leader* of that group.** This is an experience you are not familiar with. You will get feedback from the group. This may take the form of appreciative laughter or applause or come as inattentive rustling or whispering. But whether the feedback is positive or negative, you have to keep going; you have to say what you planned to say. And as long as you continue speaking, you are expected to act as if you are in charge and have everything under control.

Let's take a look at the different rules that apply to being a speaker and being an audience:

The Speaker	The Audience
• The speaker must have something to say.	• The audience doesn't have to have anything except the ability to sit upright and look in the direction of the speaker.
• The speaker stands alone in high relief.	• The audience sits together in a bunch, like peas in a pod.
• The speaker has no choice but to continue performing.	• The audience may or may not listen. At any moment a listener may turn to a neighbor and make a comment, get up and leave, glance at a newspaper, look at the ceiling, stare at a fly on the chandelier, close his or her eyes for a moment, take a nap, show boredom, indicate a lack of interest, or take out a book and read to your face.

Obviously, it is much easier to be a member of the audience. What's more, we have all been well trained in the role of audience members. At a minimum, the first twenty years of our lives have been spent as learners and receivers, as members of the audience. But there comes a point when, if we are to be successful in life, we must turn around and become teachers, givers, and leaders. We may do that well in familiar contexts—within our own families, among our associates at work, in situations that involve conversational give and take. But when asked to separate ourselves from the group, to stand alone and speak in a presentational form, many of us develop acute anxiety and begin to show the symptoms of distress noted earlier in this chapter. As Rollo May states in *Man's Search for Himself*, "Anxiety strikes us at the very core of ourselves; it is what we feel when our existence as selves is threatened." If you are one of those who have palpitations at the thought of making a speech, it is for good reason: *you have never learned to deal with the requirements of the presentational role, to make the shift from social to presentational behavior.*

In addition to a lack of training for the presentational role, we find that 65 percent of our students and clients have a history of one or more humiliating experiences that have occurred when speaking in public. Failure reinforces the fearfulness of the experience. One learns to be afraid.

The person who is afraid of speaking in public usually tries to avoid doing so. Opportunities for saying even a few words at a small meeting are passed up, so the possibility of learning a little at a time is thrown away. Avoidance leads to further avoidance, and what was merely a lack of confidence and skill becomes an actual phobia. A bad situation becomes worse.

Like Ms. C., the marketing publications illustrator, you may tell yourself it's better to keep quiet, then find you lose credit for a good idea. Or like Bill T., the sales promotion manager, you may completely "mess up" when you are put in a position where you have to speak to a group. The physical symptoms of distress become more intense. A vicious cycle is created. Afraid to speak, you do badly and, doing badly, are even more terrified the next time. You pass up the opportunity to develop your presenting behavior. But with the proper training program, that cycle can be broken.

THE SKILLS YOU NEED

Public speaking is an activity that involves mental and physical *performance skills* that are different from your social *conversational skills*.

Skills involving concentration, coordination, and quick response, both mental and physical, are just as vital to a speaker as they are to a tennis player or golfer. Your first time on the tennis court you are bound to find yourself waving your racquet at empty air or driving the ball into the net. But you want to play tennis, so you persevere and you learn. Speaking well in public also involves systematic training and practice.

There is a school of thought put forth in some books on public speaking that holds that you can be a good speaker if you just believe in yourself enough, simply psych yourself up enough beforehand. This theory suggests that confidence and poise are just a matter of willpower. But in fact confidence and poise are—and this is true in any area of life—the result of having developed the skills to carry out a task successfully.

There is no way in the world, for instance, that you can psych yourself up to drive a car in heavy city traffic if you have never been behind the wheel before. You have to start slowly and carefully, driving around the block in an uncongested area. Otherwise, no matter how hard you try, you are likely to have an accident, to lose control.

In the same sense, no matter how hard you may try to convince yourself that you can speak well in public with no training, as soon as you begin you are likely to find your throat dry, your heart racing, your memory deserting you. You are almost bound metaphorically to drive off the road.

Presenting skills are necessary, and the development of those skills requires systematic training.

The program presented in the following pages will help you to develop those skills step by step in the privacy of your own home, making use of a sequence of training exercises that will carry you all the way through the making of a speech, from the nervous moments before you begin to the final instant in which you return to your seat. You will learn how to control physical symptoms of nervousness and how to make positive use of the underlying biological impulses that cause such symptoms. A heartbeat that is more rapid than usual can be a sign of fear, but when it is under control, that same faster heartbeat can give verve and drive to your speech. Making a speech, like playing a game of tennis, is a stressful situation, and the body automatically responds to the tensions of the situation. Once you understand what your body is doing and why, you will come to understand that the symptoms you previously found to be fearful or distracting can be controlled, channeled, and put to effective use.

The skills for public speaking that can be acquired by using the Talk-Power program are as follows:

Attention skills
You will be able to shut off negative thoughts or negative stimuli coming from the audience.

Concentration skills
You will have complete command of thinking faculties, memory, and imagination.

Coordination skills
You will be able to move easily, using expressive gestures.

Self-control
You will be able to control involuntary movements such as excessive hand gesturing, head bobbing, swaying, shifting from one foot to another, and trembling.

Emotional control
You will be able to control and reduce anxiety, panic, and fear.

Fluid response
You will be able to respond clearly and comfortably to questions, interruptions, distractions, and unplanned happenings.

Warmth
You will be relaxed enough to be able to communicate qualities of humor, concern, and sincerity.

Charisma
You will be able to project an image of assurance and credibility.

Thinking on your feet

You will learn how to get rid of poor habits of mechanical memorization and instead make use of creative thinking.

Body awareness

You will learn how to become totally aware of your physical presence so that you become the center of attention for your audience.

Resistance skills

You will be able to recognize and resist the impulse to rush ahead, instead pacing yourself with control and awareness.

Vocal skills

You will learn how to keep vocal cords properly relaxed so that the voice projects with no distortion.

Imagination skills

You will be able to imagine and visualize sequences as you develop a story. You will learn to give talks without relying so completely on reading from your notes.

WHAT ABOUT RELAXATION?

You will notice that in the list of skills to be acquired, the word *relaxed* is used only once—in connection with the projection of warmth—and that even here it is a matter of becoming "relaxed *enough* to communicate qualities of humor, concern, and sincerity."

"But isn't relaxation really what it's all about?" you may ask. "My problem is that I can't relax. If I could, I'd be all right."

In fact, *relaxation is not what it's all about.* Many books on public speaking make a great to-do about relaxation, as if that alone were the key to effective public speaking. But relaxation cannot substitute for the real skills and the conditioning necessary to speaking well in public. The misconception that relaxation is the key to success in making a formal presentation almost always results in continued failure. Public speaking is a pressure situation, and advice to relax and "hang loose" is meaningless for the anxious speaker.

The reason for this is simple. In a situation in which the individual feels threatened or under unusual pressure, the body automatically responds with a heightened arousal. Thus the ability to relax is short-circuited. In addition, the state of relaxation as we usually think of it —lying in the sun and letting go of our cares—is incompatible with the task of *performing.*

Has anyone ever heard Chris Evert Lloyd say that her great backhand is the result of her ability to relax? Does Mikhail Baryshnikov claim that his miraculous leaps are the product of relaxation? Not at all. Training and skills are the necessary components. Relaxation may be great for a yoga class, but it isn't what you want in a performance situation. After all, what does relaxation really mean? A lack of tension. Speaking in public, giving a performance, always implies a certain amount of effort and a degree of tension. The brain is invariably aroused to higher levels of excitation. If we lack the ability to control that excitation, we go into a state of stress and experience feelings of fear and even pain. The heartbeat is stepped up. Sugar and red cells are released into the blood. All muscles tense to the test, the pupils dilate, the eyelids retract, even the hair bristles. Relaxing, shedding all tension, is the last thing the body is capable of in such situations.

A Chain Reaction Fear Response
(How It Builds)

Training	Stimuli	Your thoughts	Feelings	Inner response	Outer response	How this response works for you
The untrained speaker	Your boss has asked you to do a presentation for another department.	"Oh my God, I'm going to be humiliated."	fear	accelerated heartbeat, etc.; flight response	inability to work on presentation; avoidance strategies	to escape certain humiliation; to protect yourself from this threat
The trained speaker	Your boss has asked you to do a presentation for another department.	"Wow, this is my chance to show what I can do."	high excitement	rise in tension level to mobilize action	immediate preparatory work; organization of talk; rehearsal schedule	to perform the task for best results and possible rewards

THE BRAIN

To understand more fully what happens to us when we perform, whether on the tennis court or speaking before an audience, we have to take a look at the physiological composition of the brain. Most of us envision the human brain as a single entity. Actually, what we call the brain is made up of three separate brains, each of which developed independently at different stages of our evolutionary history.

The most primitive part of the human brain, located at its base, resembles the brain of reptiles, creatures whose behaviors center on survival, escape from danger, speed, strength, and the quick strike. This "reptilian" brain regulates our breathing and our heartbeat and maintains equilibrium and muscle tone.

The second brain is called the "old mammalian" brain. This brain surrounds the original reptilian brain and developed in the earliest mammals about one hundred and fifty million years ago. The old mammalian brain is the center of our emotions and sexual drives.

In the wrinkled top layers of the human brain—about an eighth of an inch thick—lies the neo-cortex, or the "new mammalian" brain. It is with this brain, commonly referred to as the *cerebral cortex,* that we think, speak, reason, and perform the many human functions that separate us from all other earthly creatures.

The cerebral cortex has a right side and a left side.

The **left side** controls:	Speech Language Logic Reason

Analysis
Serial crossing
Writing
Reading

The **right side** controls: Recognition of faces
Rhythm
Visual images—depth
Creativity
Parallel processing
Synthesis

To speak effectively in public, both sides of the cerebral cortex must be functioning freely and smoothly. But because you are in a high risk situation and feel threatened, the reptilian brain tends to take charge, revving your body up to meet the danger. Your heart beats faster, your muscles feel tense, your throat is dry, your breathing alters. This is known as the fight-or-flight response.

At the same time, your cerebral cortex seems to be shutting down. Speech, logic, and reasoning are affected. "I can't seem to think straight," you say. "I block; I get incoherent. I can't make the most obvious connections." Your reptilian brain is taking charge, sending out such strong signals that your cerebral cortex is overwhelmed and cannot function as freely as it should. This interference with your thinking process is similar to what happens when you experience indigestion that occurs when you have just eaten and are in a condition of pressure or stress. Just as with your digestive system, stress can cause a disruption in the workings of the cerebral cortex, the thinking part of your brain.

Gaining Control

Your reptilian brain needs to be brought under control. You don't want to shut off its signals altogether, though. You are giving a performance, and you need that rush of adrenaline. But you don't want the reptilian brain to take over altogether, to "override" the cerebral cortex. How can you keep the necessary and valuable impulses from the reptilian brain flowing, but at the same time control them so as to bring them into balance with the equally important functions of the cerebral cortex?

The answer lies in learning how to slow down internally. It lies in systematically training yourself, conditioning yourself to deal with the instinctive responses of the reptilian brain. You must learn deliberately to slow down those survival responses, to make them work for you instead of against you. You must learn to control your instincts to a degree that makes it possible for you to manage your level of excitement so that you are able to think on your feet.

The chapters that follow detail the training sequences that pertain to controlling your fear response through each step in making a formal or informal presentation. You will learn the physical and mental processes involved at every stage in giving a talk or a speech. Each chapter will focus on specific exercises, *behavioral training exercises,* that will teach you *how* to gain control systematically and scientifically. And all it takes is twenty minutes of practice each day for three weeks.

The wonderful part of this program is that you don't need an audience to practice the systematic exercises presented in this book. In fact, it is better not to have an audience. Even family members or close friends may become critical, without understanding what you are doing. Wait until you feel that you are handling the principles and techniques of the Talk-Power system with some degree of ease before you look for an audience.

If you do the exercises for learning concentration, control, and coordination as directed, you will find that in a surprisingly short time, your mind and body will know how to make the shift from social behavior to presentational behavior. You will be able to face an audience without panic, able to project excitement as you draw on the instinctive life force provided by the reptilian brain. At the same time, you will be able to think and talk clearly. This balanced combination is what makes human beings uniquely capable of communicating with one another through the use of emotionally expressive language.

THE TALK-POWER SYNTHESIS

One of the reasons that this program is unique is that it is based upon a synthesis of techniques drawn from three different fields.

The theoretical base of the program is behavioral. The assumption of the behavioral perspective is that one learns to be fearful, and that by zeroing in on these fearful responses through systematic training, one can learn new, more desirable responses. Just as behavior modification methods can be used to assist people who are afraid to fly or who want to give up smoking, so they can also assist in desensitizing you to your fear of speaking in public. They can help free you from bad habits that reinforce a panic reaction. For example, you will learn to read what body symptoms signal the onset of the fear response and to apply techniques that immediately stop your loss of control.

Other techniques that are used are extensions of the teachings of Stanislavsky, the great Russian theater director whose ideas inspired the Method school of acting in the United States.

"But I'm not an actor," you may be saying. So what? You don't have to have any acting talent to be able to make use of training techniques that actors use to help them concentrate and achieve a balanced use of all their thinking and speaking faculties.

The aim is not to turn you into an actor, but to enable you to speak in public without panicking. And certain theatrical training devices can be invaluable in achieving that end.

In order to achieve difficult emotional "changes," one technique used by Method actors is to walk slowly through the transitions in moment-to-moment steps. With this concept in mind, Chapter 2 will introduce you to the Present Time Exercise. This exercise guides the speaker through the most difficult transition he has to make—the transition from anonymous member of the audience to highly visible speaker standing alone.

Another Method technique known as the Sense-Memory Exercise has been redesigned into the Sense-Memory Imaging Rehearsal. This exercise will gradually condition your mind and body to cope with the shock of the presenting experience, prepare you to answer difficult questions from the floor, and teach you what it feels like to have a successful experience without taking any risks. In each chapter, you will find a schedule of practice assignments that will teach you the basic habits of rehearsal essential for a smooth professional presentation.

The third part of this synthesis has to do with the craft of speech writing.

A major cause of speaker anxiety is a lack of knowhow concerning speech construction. Several chapters of this book are devoted to speech construction, making use of our unique Talk-Power Action Formula. This formula will enable you to write a coherent and logical speech, step by step. Emphasis on crafting a speech using this unique formula provides you an additional repertory of skills overlooked in other books on public speaking.

A speech must be crafted. Because it must be delivered in a set period of time, it must be broken down into manageable sections.

The Action Formula makes use of a word budget—you learn exactly how many words should be employed to give maximum impact to each section of your speech. This word budget can be applied to a talk of any length, from six minutes to a full hour.

Familiarity with the formula gives the speaker an incomparable feeling of safety and confidence. Noam Chomsky, the world-famous psycholinguist, maintains that humans have an internal set of rules enabling them to recognize the "deep structure of a sentence." The Action Formula presents us with an external set of rules that enables us to recognize the deep structure of a speech.

THE PANIC CLINIC FOR PUBLIC SPEAKING

Even after reading this chapter you may still feel that your case is hopeless, that you will never be able to speak in public successfully. Although this program was created to help all people who are uncomfortable and fearful of speaking in public, the Panic Clinic for Public Speaking (see Appendix 1) was specifically created to help people with an extreme phobia about public speaking.

Although practically everyone has some sort of inhibition or fear about speaking in public, the Panic Clinic was originally conceived to deal with the seemingly insoluble problems of truly phobic individuals. Their stories have a common theme to them; a despairing sense that their problems are insurmountable. The Panic Clinic is often regarded as a last hope.

The systematic exercises contained in this section prepare and condition more seriously fearful individuals so that they can thereafter begin the regular Talk-Power program.

If you feel you need such basic help, turn to Appendix 1 and do the Panic Clinic exercises before going on to Chapter 2.

CHAPTER 2

Controlling Your Fear Response

You are seated, waiting to speak.

It may be that you are seated in the midst of the group that you are about to address and that you will have to rise from your chair, walk forward to the front of the group, and turn to face them before beginning to talk. Or you may be sitting in a chair on stage, facing the audience, and will need only to stand and walk forward to a podium.

I call the territory that stretches between your seat and the podium or place you stand to speak the "launching pad." Any astronaut will attest to the importance of the launching pad; any pilot will tell you that the takeoff is crucial in determining the success of a flight. If something goes wrong on the launching pad or the runway, disaster can result.

In fact, for many people who are fearful of public speaking, it is precisely here, on the launching pad, that loss of control begins. As you sit waiting to make your speech and as you get up to make your speech, it is all too easy to begin to panic. In these moments before you actually start to speak, your *unconditioned* body will show the first panicky responses to the stress of performing. The heart begins to accelerate, the palms to sweat. As you stand, you may feel dizzy; your legs may tremble.

It is essential to learn how to *slow down,* how to regain control while you are still on the launching pad. If you sit twitching nervously in your chair, stumble awkwardly to your feet, and bolt forward, beginning to speak before even taking a breath, you are going to be in trouble from the start. It may be that you will spend only two or three minutes in your seat before getting up to speak for fifteen minutes or longer. But those two or three minutes on the launching pad are so crucial that this entire chapter will be devoted to exercises that will train you to sit still and concentrate—to **resist the impulse to rush forward.** By doing these exercises, you can develop the skills necessary to make a calm, comfortable, dignified entrance. You will learn how to substitute a *coping response* for your present *fear response.*

SETTING THE STAGE

To carry out these exercises properly, you will need a quiet room without distractions. People coming in and out, a constantly ringing telephone, or a radio blaring will make it impossible to concentrate to the necessary degree. Imagine that you are about to face a group to present a talk, and try to create conditions similar to a real speaking situation.

1. Decide exactly where the audience is by placing several empty chairs in the audience section.
2. Decide where you will be sitting before you get up to give your talk. Are you sitting in the audience yourself,

or are you on a stage facing the audience? Even if you ordinarily are called on to speak while seated in a group around a table and remain sitting as you speak, you should do these exercises in full, including those involving getting up and walking forward. They will build a signal system between you and your body to train you to cope in any sort of speaking situation.

3. Place a chair in the position you decide on, and sit down.

SITTING

All of us have individual ways of sitting in a chair, although the way we sit is likely to change according to the situation. Accomplished public speakers may sit in a chair in many different ways, ways that often reveal something about their personality. But in order to train yourself to control your fear response to the stress of the performance situation, it is important to sit in the way described below, even if it does not feel natural to you at first. This is a training exercise.

Exercise One: Centering

1. Be aware of the weight of your body in the chair.

Try to sit so that your body is evenly balanced, with equal weight on the right and left buttocks.

2. Be sure that your stomach muscles are relaxed.

3. Feel your body weight sinking downward in one direction.

Once you have achieved a feeling of being centered, you can move on to the second exercise.

Exercise Two: Concentration

Anxiety in a performance situation is directly related to a lack of concentration. This exercise is designed to train you to tune out distractions, including the audience, and keep your attention focused inward. Do this exercise remaining in your centered position in your chair.

1. Shake your hands vigorously twenty times.
2. Stop.
3. Place your hands in your lap.
4. Concentrate on the tingling feeling (or the pulse) in your fingertips. Focus your attention as much as possible on that pulse.
5. Concentrate on your fingertips for ten seconds. (If your body is tense or your heart is still beating rapidly, don't worry about it at this point.)
6. Keep your eyes gently open but unfocused, looking straight ahead as you concentrate on your fingertips.

If you find it difficult to carry out these two exercises, you will need to begin with even more fundamental techniques for getting in touch with your body. Turn at once to Appendix 1. Here you will find the Panic Clinic for Public Speaking. This special section contains several very simple exercises for those with severe panic reactions.

Note: Shaking the hands is a preliminary exercise and can be dispensed with after the second week of training.

STANDING

The faster you respond, the more you will lose control.

The purpose of the following exercise is to teach you to resist the impulse to bolt out of your chair and rush to the front of the platform or group. Resistance skills can only be acquired through systematic practice. You have to *train* your body to slow down. It is useless to promise yourself that next time you won't rush—useless because the fight-or-flight response associated with the survival instincts of the "reptilian brain" discussed in Chapter 1 is simply too powerful and too automatic. Learning how to slow down and hold back physically will help you combat the feeling that you are losing control and to conquer the panic that goes with that feeling.

Exercise Three: Slow Motion Stand

Every step in this exercise should be done as deliberately as though you had been filmed in slow motion.

1. Sitting in your chair, concentrate on your fingertips.
2. Still concentrating on your fingertips, slowly push your body forward in your chair.
3. *Very slowly,* your knees still bent, use the bottom of your feet and your legs to ease yourself off your chair, almost in a crouching position. Let your arms hang at your sides. (Yes, this is a very clumsy way to get out of a chair, but its very awkwardness is its point. It makes it impossible for you to bolt out of your chair.)
4. Now straighten your knees *very slowly* as you bring your body up to a standing position. Keep your hands at your sides, and straighten your head last.
5. Be sure that your stomach muscles are relaxed.

6. You are now standing in place in front of your chair. Concentrate on your fingertips. Try to feel the weight of your body perfectly balanced on both feet.
7. Stand still, eyes straight ahead but unfocused.

Exercise Four: Balance Awareness

As you stand in place *before* beginning to walk, make sure that the weight of your trunk is evenly distributed between your right foot and your left foot. Your head should be perfectly centered between your right and left shoulders. But it is not enough merely to position yourself in this balanced stance; you must *feel* it, become fully aware of it. Take a moment to sense fully the balance you have achieved.

The effect of developing such balance awareness goes beyond the matter of grounding yourself. Students and clients have repeatedly confirmed that achievement of balance awareness has the additional benefit of *slowing down an accelerated heartbeat,* thus stopping the automatic fear response so many people experience when faced with the stress of speaking in public. Indeed, the racing of the heart is often cut by one third to one half. At the same time, more normal breathing ensues. This presumably occurs because the reptilian brain regulates the heartbeat and breathing as well as muscle-tone and equilibrium. Gaining control of one's equilibrium (balance) through awareness seems to act as an inhibitor to a rapid heartbeat and uncontrolled breathing.

Standing still and taking the few seconds to achieve balance awareness before you begin to walk is vitally important. In addition, this act of awareness strengthens your control, making you able to hold on to your concentration as you begin to move.

Exercise Five: Walking

The purpose of this exercise is to train you to retain control and concentration even when you are in motion. The faster you move, the more control you lose.

Stand in place in front of your chair with equal weight on both feet, concentrating on the perfect balance of your body. Now:

- Take a step with your right foot.
- Take a step with your left foot.
- Stop with both feet on the ground.
- Concentrate on your fingertips.
- Take a step with your right foot.
- Take a step with the left foot.
- Stop with both feet on the ground.
- Concentrate on your fingertips.

Repeat this cycle as many times as necessary to bring you to the front of the stage or to the point where you will turn to face your audience if you have been sitting among the group.

If you feel like a robot doing this exercise, fine. You should. In the slowness of the forward movement lies the secret of control. Once you have trained yourself to resist the impulse to rush, you will be able to walk normally without stopping, while at the same time you retain complete inner attention and focus. You also will find that your heart has stopped beating so rapidly.

As you practice this exercise, *do not*

- Bounce
- Sway

- Jiggle
- Touch your hair
- Touch your body
- Touch your clothes
- Bob your head
- Put your hands in your pockets

FACING THE AUDIENCE

If you have been sitting in the audience itself, you will have to turn to face the group after completing your walk forward. *Turn slowly.* If you have been sitting on stage and have walked forward toward the audience, come to a full stop.

Now that you are facing your audience, what is the next thing that you do?

Do you adjust your clothes?

Do you clear your throat?

Do you begin to speak immediately?

No.

You are now in a totally new position in relation to the audience. You need a moment to adjust to that position, and the audience needs a moment to take you in, to adjust to you. As you look out over the audience, the sight of all those faces looking back at you can easily stimulate a fresh wave of anxiety. If you begin your speech immediately, you may find yourself losing control. Your knees may tremble, or there may be a tremor in your voice. If you rush forward without pausing, you may get ahead of your thoughts, with a resultant blocking of ideas.

Allow yourself a ten- to fifteen-second "period of adjustment." During these few seconds, there are three things that must occur:

1. Your body must find a comfortable balance in this new position.
2. Your muscles must adjust from a moving tension to a standing-still equilibrium. (We call this *grounding yourself*.)
3. Your eyes must adjust to whatever changes in lighting your new position may involve and to the changed spatial relationship between you and your audience.

How, you may ask, can I just stand there, letting these adjustments take place while the audience is looking at me and waiting for me to speak?

Well, for one thing, the audience actually expects a momentary pause. They have seen the pianist at a concert pause before raising his hands to the keys, they have seen baseball players do it when coming to bat, and they are aware that the experienced speaker will pause also before beginning his or her presentation.

In order to ground yourself emotionally, as well as physically, it is necessary to take stock of exactly how you feel during those moments before you begin your speech. It is likely that you will be feeling some physical and emotional discomfort. Such discomfort is in itself frightening to many people. They attempt to deny or blank out what they are feeling, what is in fact happening to them. They begin their speech immediately, rushing into it. The trouble is that they are totally out of contact with their bodies.

The following Present Time Exercise will train you to take inventory of what you are feeling. The few moments it takes to do the exercise will automatically create that vital pause before you speak.

Exercise Six: Present Time Inventory

When first practicing this coping exercise in private, you should *speak out loud as you go through the checklist* and select the response that best describes how you feel. Later, when you face an actual audience, you will of course go through the checklist silently in your mind. (This exercise eventually will take no more than three seconds.)

Checklist

My head feels	dizzy . . . heavy . . . light . . . clear
My eyes are	blurry . . . staring . . . tearing . . . steady
My mouth is	clenched . . . trembling . . . dry . . . moist
My throat feels	dry . . . raspy . . . tight
My neck is	tight . . . tense
My shoulders are	tight . . . tense . . . slumping . . . straight
My heart is	pounding . . . racing . . . normal
My chest is	tight . . . pounding . . . heaving
My arms are	hanging at my sides . . . jerking . . . heavy
My hands are	twitching . . . hot . . . cold . . . clenched . . . loose
My legs are	weak . . . swaying . . . unstable . . . steady
My knees are	shaking . . . locked . . . stable
My feet are	unbalanced . . . balanced

In doing this exercise, try not to think in negative terms. For example, instead of saying "My head feels awful," try to identify the specific sensation that you are feeling in your head—"My head feels heavy . . . light . . . tight." The point here is not to pass judgment on how you feel, but simply to be in touch with how you feel. If you "read" and acknowledge how you feel, you will be better able to control your responses.

The person who plunges into a speech without taking inventory, trying to deny the uncomfortable things that are going on in his or her body, invariably encounters the most severe mental blocking. The reason for this is that it takes so much effort and energy to cut your awareness off from what your body is experiencing that a lot of tension is produced. This tension seems to interfere with the normal functioning of the cerebral cortex (the thinking-speaking part of your brain), and the result is thought and speech blocking.

I have designed the Present Time Exercise so that you will learn how to **make your mind and body work together.** This unity of function creates the inner conditions that will deepen your concentration. In my seminars I have seen hundreds of people with the most severe thought-blocking problems learn to speak without hesitation in a matter of days by practicing the body awareness exercises introduced in this chapter.

EYE CONTACT

In my classes and seminars, the exercises set forth here are practiced in front of other class members. There is one final element involved in facing an audience that invariably comes up at this point. Even though you are doing the exercises in private and your audience is purely imaginary, the following question will probably also occur to you: *Should you make eye contact with an audience before you begin to speak?*

The answer, you may be surprised to learn, is *no*—at least not in the way you may think.

As discussed in Chapter 1, there are significant differences between social conversation and speaking to an audience. Those differences extend to what is loosely called eye contact. In a social conversation, it is usual (and preferable) to look directly into the eyes of your listener or the person who is speaking to you from time to time. You have probably had the unnerving experience of conversing with someone who always looks just over your shoulder, as though speaking to someone standing behind you. In social conversation such a habit is unsettling because it breaks the lines of intimate give and take. But when you are speaking to an audience, there is no such give and take. Even in circumstances in which the speaker takes questions from members of the audience, the answers you give must be addressed to the audience as a whole, not merely to the individual questioner.

Do not try to fix your eyes on the eyes of audience members. When you first begin to speak your high level of excitement causes your eyes to dilate. If you try to focus on any specific person or thing at a distance, this will cause enormous strain and tension on your eyes, which can easily add to the emotional stress of the moment. Rather, *look in the general direction of* the faces in your audience, neither too high above their heads or so low that you appear to be looking at the floor. As your speech progresses, you can move your head slowly to the left or right from time to time, so that you take in the entire room, keeping your gaze at the eye level of the audience but without fixing anyone with an actual direct stare.

If it should happen that you make contact simultaneously with someone's eyes, or if you notice that an audience member is showing particular interest in what you are saying, then by all means give such a person more attention. But do not stare and do not keep your eyes on one individual for more than a few seconds at a time. If you actively stare into the eyes of audience members, they will feel that you are pursuing them. *No audience will tolerate being pursued. It is up to them to come to you.* You and what you have to say should be the center of attention. In fact, if you simply look in the general direction of the faces of your audience, moving your head to take in various parts of the room at different times, most members of the audience will have the feeling that you are speaking to them personally, even though you have not once looked anyone directly in the eyes. So stop worrying about eye contact.

And now it is time for you to begin to speak.

CHAPTER 3

How to Begin Talking

The inexperienced, untrained speaker may encounter a variety of problems when first beginning a speech. One person may talk much too fast, another may stutter hesitantly, while a third speaks just above a whisper in an almost inaudible voice. Once again, overcoming such problems is a matter of training, of taking things step by step.

The best way to train yourself to begin a speech confidently and smoothly is to practice with a simple uncomplicated story—a short, but complete story that has a beginning, a middle, and an end. In other words, tell a joke or relate a humorous anecdote.

"But I'm terrible at telling jokes," you may object.

Even if that's the case, the telling of a joke or anecdote remains the best method for training yourself to begin a speech. When the time comes for you to give an actual speech before a real audience, you can begin your speech in a number of other ways if you don't feel comfortable telling a joke. But as a training exercise, the telling of a joke has proved remarkably effective in my classes and seminars. (You don't have to worry about writing out a script for yourself at this point. A selection of jokes given to me by my students has been provided for you at the end of this chapter. Or, if you're good at telling jokes, you can use one of your own.)

The joke you select should be no more than 150 words —approximately one minute of speaking time. It should be no less than 75 words, however. It should have a definite conclusion, a punch line. It should be a story that is as pictorial as possible, avoiding mood descriptions and theoretical or philosophical abstractions.

This training exercise is carried out in two parts. First read the joke aloud. Then tell it again, trying to recall it without looking at your notes. Begin by picking a joke from the selection offered at the end of the chapter or by making use of a favorite of your own. Print or type the joke on a 5 × 8 index card, skipping every other line so that you can read it easily. It should look something like the following example:

> AS A FRESHMAN AT A WESTERN COLLEGE, MY SON WAS FILLING OUT A QUESTIONNAIRE DURING ORIENTATION WEEK. A FRIEND SITTING NEXT TO HIM SEEMED TO HAVE COME TO THE END OF HIS ROPE AS FAR AS QUESTIONNAIRES WERE CONCERNED. WHEN HE CAME TO THE QUESTION "DO YOU BELIEVE IN COLLEGE MARRIAGES?" HE SHRUGGED AND OBLIGINGLY WROTE: "YES, IF THE COLLEGES REALLY LOVE EACH OTHER."

When you practice telling your joke, you're not going to tell your joke cold, of course. You're going to lead up to it by going through the sitting, standing, balance awareness, walking, and grounding exercises described in the previous chapter.

Exercise Seven: Rehearsal

1. Take your card into your rehearsal space (the place where you had decided to practice your presentation).
2. Sit in your chair, focus inward, and center yourself.
3. Put your card in your lap and shake your hands vigorously (twenty shakes).
4. Concentrate on the tingling in your fingertips.
5. Take your card in your hand.
6. Very slowly pull yourself up to your feet.
7. Stand in place and balance your weight evenly on both feet.
8. Step forward—right foot, left foot; stop on both feet. Concentrate on your fingertips. Continue forward, concentrating on your fingertips. Remember to walk very slowly. Resist the impulse to rush ahead.
9. Repeat the procedure until you have reached the point from which you will be speaking.
10. If you have walked forward from a seat in the audience, turn *slowly* to face the audience, your arms at your sides.
11. Carefully and slowly focus your attention on each part of your body. Say out loud: My head feels . . .

My eyes are . . .
My mouth is . . .
My shoulders are . . .
My neck is . . .
My chest feels . . .
My heart is . . .
My arms are . . .
My stomach is . . .
My hands feel . . .
My legs are . . .
My knees are . . .
My feet are . . .

12. Read your joke out loud in a normal voice. Don't whisper or strain for volume.

13. When you finish reading your joke, determine which part of your body feels most uncomfortable, and then name that part of your body out loud.

14. Now walk back to your seat slowly and sit quietly while you take ten gentle breaths. (A breath is one inhalation plus one exhalation. Gently breathe in through the nostrils and slowly blow out through the mouth.) Then stand up again and repeat the entire routine until ten minutes have passed. For the second part of this exercise, do exactly the same thing, including all steps, but this time try to tell your joke from memory, without using your card.

If you have any trouble remembering your joke, stop. Wait and concentrate on your fingertips for the slow count of five. Do not go back to the beginning of the joke. Then continue from the point where you broke off.

Exercise Seven should be done every day for a week. Each day pick a different joke to tell. If you were to use the same joke every day, you might well become proficient at telling that particular story, but you would learn less. This is a training exercise. By using a different joke or anecdote each day, you will not only stretch yourself more, but will also be able to recognize more fully the progress you are making in developing a command of the techniques involved. It isn't the joke itself that is important. What you are learning is a method of presenting yourself successfully to an audience.

To help you keep track of your progress, after each training session fill in the schedule that follows. By the end of a week you should find this exercise increasingly easy. The rating you give yourself should have moved to a "calmer" position.

Schedule

Day	Joke #	Time—start/finish	Comments	Rate yourself (calm) 1 to 10 (nervous)
Example	#11	7:30/7:50	Very difficult	7
1				
2				
3				
4				
5				
6				
7				

SPECIAL EXERCISES

Now that you have had an opportunity to do a real live rehearsal, you might like to know what to do about:

- Loss of control
- Forgetting the first words of a talk
- Talking too fast
- Nonverbal fillers
- Moving your hands
- Grounding yourself
- The bobbing head habit
- Breathing

Special Exercise A: Recovering Control

The beginning speaker often experiences a general loss of control at some point during his speech. If you find that you begin to lose control midway through your joke, it is probably because your level of excitement is going up too quickly. There is only one thing to do. *Stop talking.* Take a pause of three or four seconds, concentrating on your fingertips.

It is important to *take that pause the moment you feel yourself beginning to lose control.* If you wait too long, the loss of control will have gone so far that you risk complete loss of your equilibrium, and it will be more difficult for you to regain your composure.

Here is a step-by-step breakdown of this technique. Let us assume that you are in the middle of your joke or anecdote. Your heart is beginning to beat very quickly, or you are starting to breathe in a gasping manner.

1. Stop at the end of your sentence.
2. Immediately concentrate on your fingertips.
3. Count to yourself—"one hundred winners, two hundred winners, three hundred winners, four hundred winners"—looking in the direction of your audience as you do so.
4. Resume the telling of your joke. Once again, *always continue from where you left off.*

Special Exercise B: Recalling the First Words of Your Talk

Whenever you speak to a group, whether standing before them or addressing them at the conference table or in class, there is an implied physical as well as psychological *distance.* The intimacy of the one-on-one experience is gone because you are in the presentational mode.

Remember that the thinking part of your brain is divided into two hemispheres, the right brain and the left brain. It is the function of the right brain to make all the adjustments in spatial relationships. The left brain deals more with words, language, and abstraction.

I've observed hundreds of people blank out when about to deliver their opening remarks. My theory is that the problem of blanking out often arises because you are trying to perform a left brain function (recalling the specific words of your talk) while your right brain is still busily involved in making the proper adjustments to the new spatial relationship between you and the audience. As a result there is interference with the normal left brain (word recall) function, and this seems to trigger the loss of memory.

If you do have difficulty remembering the first words of your talk, the best thing to do is imagine or visualize, because imaging is a right brain function. Think in terms of picturing the scene where your joke or story begins to happen. In other words, try to see the place where your story begins. If your story takes place in a field or on a train, instead of thinking the word *field* or *train,* try to see a picture of a field or train. Then begin telling your story or joke just as you had planned.

Here is an example of how you could change a story so that instead of beginning with abstract words, you begin with words that imply pictures. First, the story with abstract words at the beginning.

They say that you should try to use patience when dealing with children.

A man was with his child and the child was misbehaving, causing a scene. Amazingly, the father remained very calm and kept saying, "Michael, take it easy. Control yourself, Michael." Finally a woman approached the distressed man and said, "You know, I am a teacher in a special education school, and I must say I admire your self-control. I might add that you have a fine looking lad. Is his name Michael?" "No," the father answered, "his name isn't Michael. I happen to be Michael. This is Johnny."

Now see how by simply changing the first line you can make it much easier to remember how your story begins.

A man was taking a walk with his child in Central Park. The child was kicking and screaming and carrying on, causing a scene. Amazingly, the father remained very calm and kept saying, "Michael, take it easy. Michael, control yourself." Finally a woman approached the distressed man and said, "You know, I am a teacher in a special education school, and I must say that I admire your self-control. I might add that you have a fine looking lad. Is his name Michael?" The father answered, "No, his name isn't Michael. I happen to be Michael."

Incredible as it may seem, by simply imagining the scene in Central Park and the child kicking and screaming when you begin, you will help activate your right brain functions so that the words to your story can follow as fluently and easily as they normally do. Whenever you are stuck and cannot remember a thought, try to picture the action behind the thought rather than grasp for the words. You will have a much better chance of recalling what it is that you wanted to say.

Special Exercise C: Talking Too Fast

Aside from loss of control, one of the most common faults displayed by the untrained speaker is talking too fast. The exercises in Chapter 2, which focus on training you to move more slowly and deliberately, will, with repetition, have a carry-over effect on your tendency to speak too quickly as well. But there is an additional technique you can make use of once you have actually begun to talk, if you still are speaking too quickly.

When you write your joke on your card, every time you come to the end of a sentence put a line like this ________ after the period. Your card will have five, six, or even seven such lines on it.

While reading your joke, stop whenever you see one of these lines and count to yourself, "one line, two lines, three lines," before continuing on to the next sentence. Using this technique causes even the most frantic speakers to begin to slow down eventually. How long will it take? It depends on the individual, of course. It can take as little as two weeks. But since you are trying to break the habits of a lifetime, it can sometimes take much longer. Even if it takes months, the results are worth the effort. Many "speed-talkers" who have used this technique have reported that it has also had an effect on their tendency to talk too fast in ordinary conversations. Without even thinking about it, they eventually found themselves pausing at appropriate moments, keeping their speech patterns under control. They broke an old habit and replaced it with a new and more appropriate one.

Special Exercise D: Inhibiting Nonverbal Fillers

The use of nonverbal fillers such as *er, ah,* and *umm* can also be a problem for inexperienced—and sometimes even well-seasoned—speakers. For many people, it is extremely discomfiting to have even a half second of silence elapse while they are speaking in public. Instead of stopping to think in silence, such people develop a nervous habit of making nonverbal sounds to fill the pause. This may comfort the speaker, but it often drives an audience wild with irritation.

In most cases, individuals who make use of the TalkPower program get over this habit without special attention. The elimination of nonverbal fillers is a natural byproduct of the training system itself, not only because of the focus on body awareness and self-mastery that has been discussed so far, but also because the speechwriting formula to be described in subsequent chapters makes it possible for the speaker to know exactly where he or she is in a speech at any given moment.

However, if you feel that the use of nonverbal fillers is a severe problem for you, and one that you want to tackle head-on, you can work at extinguishing this habit through the following techniques adapted from the behavior modification repertoire. The point of this technique is to make yourself so acutely aware of a habit you wish to get rid of that you begin automatically to inhibit the tendency.

You will need a tape recorder, a pencil, and a piece of paper for completing this special exercise.

1. Make a tape recording of yourself doing a brief talk.
2. Play the recording back. Every time you hear yourself say "er," "ah," or "umm," make a mark on your paper as follows: ////.
3. Now repeat the talk without the tape recorder, while standing up as though addressing an audience. Every time you hear yourself making an unnecessary verbal noise to fill a pause, make a mark on your paper. You will probably find that at first you are using nonverbal fillers more than ever. But that is part of the point—you want to *become fully aware of what you are doing.*
4. Each time you feel the impulse to use a nonverbal filler, take a deep breath instead, and blow the air *slowly* out through your mouth.
5. Repeat the procedure for five days, using the tape recorder first, and then going through the talk two more times without the tape recorder. Take a five-minute break between each repetition.
6. After five days, the number of marks you make on your paper will have decreased significantly. Continue the exercise for a second week, working on it every other day. If necessary, the procedure can be repeated for a third week, but that is seldom necessary.

Special Exercise E: Controlling Your Hands/Grounding Yourself

Just as many people begin a speech by talking much too fast, it is common for the untrained speaker to start moving his hands and his body in general the moment he begins to speak. This is usually a mistake. Many people who insist on moving their arms at the beginning of a speech invariably flap and wave and jerk about in a manner that looks awkward and tense. This is extremely distracting to the audience.

Therefore, when beginning to speak, always try to keep your hands at your sides during the minute it takes to tell your joke or anecdote. Practice this as an exercise when you rehearse your presentation.

"But I'm used to moving my arms," you may say. You may in fact feel more comfortable moving your arms and gesturing with your hands. You may feel, as many of my students put it, "like a zombie," with your arms hanging at your sides. But you won't look like a zombie if you keep your arms at your sides. You will look calm and collected. If you insist upon moving your hands too soon, regardless of how comfortable you may feel, you will look awkward.

"But aren't I supposed to feel comfortable?" you may ask. "Isn't that the whole point?"

No, that isn't the whole point. Not at all. The object is to give the audience the impression that you are comfortable, whether you are or not, and to help you to live with any feelings of discomfort as you successfully accomplish your task. Comfort comes when your talk is over and you know that you have done well. The feelings of pleasure from your success will cause your fearful feelings to disappear gradually.

Very often in seminars, when I ask a speaker how he

feels about standing up in front of the group, he will say that his knees are shaky or that his voice is wobbly. In almost every instance, there is no indication of this to the class. It is very important to understand that although you may *feel* nervous and shaky, if you are using body awareness techniques, thus keeping your body still and under control, none of the nervous symptoms you *feel* will be obvious to your audience. As a matter of fact, you will *look* calm and pulled together.

When you are giving a presentation, you feel you are in a stressful situation. Uncontrolled movements, even if they make you feel more comfortable, will invariably give you away. To the audience, flapping hands and a bobbing head will look uncontrolled and indicate to them that you are nervous.

When we are conversing socially with people we know well, we hardly notice the involuntary jerks, tics, and spasms of their bodies. But when we meet someone for the first time, we are much more aware of such movements. "She seems nervous," we say to ourselves, or, "He certainly is hyper." In most cases, when you are making a speech, the majority of the audience is meeting you for the first time. Each person in the audience is going to be very aware of your initial demeanor. Unless you are highly trained—a professional actor perhaps—if you begin to use your arms the moment you begin speaking, the gestures you use will be involuntary and will look hectic and uncontrolled.

There is a distinct difference between *involuntary movements* and *expressive gestures.*

Involuntary movements are spastic jerks, tics, hand waving, etc. that are in no way connected to the meaning of what the speaker is saying. These movements are simply manifestations of uncontrolled nervousness.

Expressive gestures are hand, arm, facial, or body movements that further express the speaker's meaning to the audience. Expressive gestures enhance a talk, and the ability to use them appropriately as a mode of communication comes from much experience. Beginning speakers are advised to keep their movements as simple as possible.

Grounding Yourself

There are basic, natural laws that affect us all in terms of the way we move. No matter how slowly you have walked across the floor to the podium or the front of the group you are addressing, your body has been in motion. You have used different muscles than the ones under tension while you were sitting. Your internal organs have shifted, however slightly, as you walked. As a result, *your body needs to be grounded* again before you can have full control over its movements. You need to adjust to the new experience of standing still in one place. If you begin to speak immediately, before that grounding process is complete, you will be out of control. Your chest and shoulders will tighten up because the muscles haven't had time to adjust to your new physical circumstances. As a result, any movement you do make will probably be slightly jerky and tense.

On the other hand, if you *begin to speak with your arms hanging loosely at your sides,* the gentle downward pull of your arms will cause the muscles of your arm sockets and chest to relax. It will only take sixty seconds or so for this to happen, just about the time it takes to tell your joke or humorous anecdote. Only then will you be ready to use conscious, voluntary, deliberately expressive body movements or gestures that act out, illustrate, or further communicate the message or meaning you as speaker want to get across. So again, when you begin speaking keep your hands hanging at your sides while telling your joke. Train yourself to begin speaking *without* using your arms and hands.

Special Exercise F: Breaking the Bobbing Head Habit

One of the symptoms of lack of physical control is an excessively bobbing head when presenting. It is as if the speaker were using his head instead of his hands to express himself. A bobbing head is not only a distraction for the audience, it also diminishes the speaker's image of professionalism and thus his credibility. If you have any doubt about this, just stand in front of a mirror and watch yourself make a statement as you bob your head, then do the same thing holding your head still. Even if your head feels stiff and unnatural you will have to admit that you look much more effective with a head that is under control.

The most serious effect of a bobbing head, however, is that when your neck muscles tense up and your head begins to move about with force, your chest clenches up like a fist. You stop breathing normally, thereby cutting down on the amount of air that you are taking in. This causes a gasping breathlessness that seriously interferes with optimal performance.

Here is an exercise that I have designed for students and clients who wish to break the bobbing head habit. Do the exercise for five minutes once a day for four weeks. At the end of the four weeks, rest for one week and begin again if the condition is still not under control.

Usually four weeks will do the job.

1. Stand with your back against the wall.
2. Feel your head gently pressing against the wall.

3. Concentrate on this feeling of your head gently pressing against the wall, and remember to breathe normally.

4. Hold a page from a newspaper in front of your eyes and read one article out loud. Read slowly, do not move your head. The point is to keep your awareness on the feeling of your head as it presses against the wall while you read. Do not forget to breathe normally.

If you have to do a presentation, rehearse your talk in this way. You may feel stiff and zombielike, but remember this is a training device. You are trying to break an undesirable habit by introducing a more desirable way of holding your head.

As time goes by, your new control will become more and more a part of your normal behavior and you will no longer feel stiff, but poised and comfortable.

Special Exercise G: Regulating Your Breathing

The implementation of the Talk-Power system begins with the development of centering, body awareness, and balance awareness. Once you have developed your skills in these areas and are up on your feet, it will be easier for you to make use of specific breathing techniques. Just as you can influence the rate of your heartbeat by concentrating on your sense of inner balance, so you can reduce your level of anxiety by learning to regulate your breathing.

Let's start by looking at how your breathing processes are controlled by the *autonomic nervous system.* Governed by your reptilian brain, the autonomic nervous system is composed of two separate subsidiary systems.

The *sympathetic* nervous system regulates bodily

arousal, including the rapid heartbeat and quick breathing experienced under stress.

The *parasympathetic* nervous system regulates inhibitory functions and slows down the rate of arousal.

In *The Human Nervous System,* David Jensen states: "A generalized activation of the sympathetic system prepares the individual for intense muscular activity such as is required in defense or offense, the so called fight or flight reaction." Parasympathetic activity, on the other hand, "is concerned primarily with mechanisms responsible for maintaining *resting* bodily functions such as reducing the heart rate, promotion of digestive activities, . . ." etc.

These two systems work together. Either one or the other is dominant at a given time in the body. When you have to get up to give a presentation and you become anxious, it is your sympathetic nervous system that is speeding up your heart and sending you fear signals.

But if you can get your parasympathetic system to work for you when you are feeling highly frightened and nervous, you can, as easily as pressing a button, inhibit or stop your fear response.

At this point you may be asking, "How can one do this if these two systems are a part of the autonomic system, involving automatic responses over which we have no control?"

The answer is that these systems are not completely involuntary. As Jensen goes on to say, "It is now clear that a number of supposedly involuntary processes are indeed subject to modification by application of conscious mental effort on the part of the subject." Thus when you deliberately focus attention on your breathing behavior and regulate that breathing by inhaling slowly through your nostrils and exhaling slowly through your mouth, you can inhibit your fear response. The reason for this is that with slow breathing the parasympathetic system (inhibitory function) becomes dominant and you decrease the sympathetic system (arousal).

The breath regulating exercise that teaches you how to begin to break the habit of fear response breathing is a very simple one. It will introduce calm breathing into your repertoire of presentational skills.

1. Sit in a chair. Center yourself—that is, focus inward and make sure that your weight is evenly balanced between your right and left buttock. Feel that your head is comfortably balanced between your right and left shoulder. Let go of all tension and gently close your eyes. Stay focused inward and now become aware of your breathing.
2. Place your hands just below your ribs, across your belly. As you breathe, the intake of air should cause a slight expansion of your belly. The expansion is caused by the sheet of muscle called the diaphragm pushing down to make room for the inhaled air. When you exhale, you will feel your belly contract a little as the diaphragm pushes the breath up and out of your lungs. This is called diaphragmatic breathing.
3. As you become aware of this rhythm, concentrate on the tip of your nose and, through the nostrils, breathe in a long gentle breath to the count of four; then, through the mouth, blow out a gentle exhalation to the count of four. Check to see that you are not becoming tense while you are doing this exercise. Do this breathing and silent counting ten times. Each time you inhale and blow out constitutes one complete breath.
4. After you have done ten complete breaths with your eyes closed, stay focused inward but open your eyes gradually. Do not blink or try to look at anything directly.

Just keep a "soft eye" and continue breathing in this slow gentle way, counting as you breathe. Do another set of ten inhalations and ten exhalations. Counting is very important because it holds your attention on yourself and keeps you feeling grounded or rooted. It is perfectly possible to do this with your eyes open, fully aware of what is going on around you, yet with 75 percent of your attention focused on your calming technique.

This breath regulating technique can be used anywhere at any time to help you calm yourself. It is virtually undetectable to an observer. You just sit quietly on the speaker's platform with your hands lightly folded across your belly, breathing slowly in and out.

This technique is invaluable for overcoming *hyperventilation,* the rapid shallow breathing that accompanies a fear response in stressful situations. When you hyperventilate, the air is not pulled down into your diaphragm area; you will not feel the expansion and contraction of your belly. Instead, your chest will be heaving as you inhale and exhale at a rapid rate. In his book *Stop Running Scared,* Dr. Herbert Fensterheim describes the results of hyperventilation: "When you become anxious your breathing changes so that it becomes more shallow. Just as when you pant during physical exercise, this builds up excess oxygen, in your blood. During heavy exercise you use up this excess oxygen; during your fear response, you do not use it up. As a result, it changes the acid-alkaline balance in the blood and consequently brings on the changes of body feeling the dizziness, heart palpitations feeling of weakness in the knees. These intensify the fear reaction and may prove a source of fear in themselves."

The breathing exercises above will help to overcome

hyperventilation should it occur. But it should be emphasized that the likelihood of hyperventilation will be greatly reduced in the first place if the exercises for developing concentration, body awareness, and balance awareness are performed on a daily basis. Breathing exercises are a useful adjunct to the basic program, but they cannot substitute for the step-by-step development of the skills discussed earlier in this chapter and Chapter 2.

SAMPLE JOKES/ANECDOTES

The following is a small collection of jokes and anecdotes to be used for practicing Exercise Seven (your daily rehearsal for learning to talk fluently).

It was early in the morning in John's bedroom, and his mother was trying to wake him up. "John," she said, "John, it's late. You must get out of bed to go to school." "No," said John. "I don't want to go to school." "Well," said his mother, "I'm willing to listen to why you won't go to school, if you will listen to me tell you why you should."

"Mother," said John, "I hate school because the kids don't like me. They throw spitballs at me and push me down the stairs. I don't want to go."

"All right," said his mother, "now I'll tell you why you should get up to go to school. John, you are fifty-three years old and the principal of that high school. Get up right now or you'll be late for the morning assembly."

A man getting his hair cut said to the barber, "I want you to use the clippers on the right side and clip close and high. On the left side, don't use the clippers—leave the hair long so it'll cover my ear. On top, near the crown, make a bald spot about the size of a silver dollar. Also on top, leave a long, narrow wisp that I can pull down over my nose and have it touch my chin."

With that the barber said, "But, mister, I can't cut hair like that."

"I don't see why not!" the man shouted. "That's the way you cut it the last time."

Three squaws in a remote Indian tribe were pregnant and due to deliver at about the same time. According to an old tribal tradition each squaw had to go out, kill an animal, and then bear her child on the animal's hide. The child would then exhibit all the strong characteristics of that animal.

The first squaw, when time drew near, killed a lion and bore a strong, brave son.

The second squaw killed a tiger and bore a strong, brave son.

The third squaw killed a hippopotamus and bore twin sons, both strong and brave.

The moral of the story: The squaw of the hippopotamus equals the sons of the squaws of the other two hides.

When her daughters were very small girls, Mrs. Dwight Morrow gave a high tea at which one of the guests was to be the senior J. P. Morgan. The girls were to be brought in, introduced, and ushered out. Mrs. Morrow's great fear was the possibility that Anne, the most outspoken of them, might comment audibly upon Mr. Morgan's celebrated and conspicuous nose. She therefore took pains beforehand to explain to Anne that personal observations were impolite and cautioned her especially against making any comment upon Mr. Morgan's nose, no matter what she might think of it.

When the moment came and the children were brought in, Mrs. Morrow held her breath as she saw Anne's gaze fix upon the banker's most prominent facial feature and remain there. Nonetheless, the introduction was made without incident. The little girls curtsied politely and were sent on their way. With a sigh of relief, Mrs. Morrow turned back to her duties as hostess and inquired of her guest, "And now, Mr. Morgan, will you have cream or lemon in your nose?"

Two carrots, a boy and a girl, are walking together down the street, hand in hand. As they come to a corner, the girl carrot steps down off the sidewalk into the street just as a car comes careening around the corner. There's a squeal of the car's brakes, but the car nevertheless runs right over her.

An ambulance rushes her to the hospital. The boy carrot is extremely upset. What's going to happen to his friend? Will she be all right?

In the hospital, the boy carrot sees the doctor coming towards him down the hall. With a grim look, the doctor comes up to him and says, "My friend, I've got some news for you—good news and bad news. I'll give you the good news first. Your friend is going to live, but—and I'm sorry—she's going to be a vegetable for the rest of her life."

A young man who had never been sick before in his life has just gotten over a very serious illness. The experience has left him shaken, because now for the first time he realizes that he is mortal. He tells his doctor, "I am willing to do anything if it will help me to live a long life. Tell me, what must I do?"

The doctor says, "Get up early, don't stay up late, eat plenty of leafy vegetables, don't smoke, don't drink, stay away from women."

"If I do all those things," asks the young man, "will I really live longer?"

"No," replies the doctor, "but it will seem a lot longer."

Two neighbors were having coffee while one was preparing dinner for guests that evening.

She took a leg of lamb out of the refrigerator and proceeded to cut off the end bone with a saw.

Her neighbor asked why she was doing this. She replied, "I guess . . . well, I really don't know. My mother always prepared her leg of lamb that way. I think I'll call her and ask."

The mother's reply was, "I really don't know either. Your grandmother always did it that way. I'll call and ask her."

The grandmother's answer was, "It was the only solution I could think of. My favorite pot was too small."

A patient came into his doctor's office and said, "I've got a real bad pain in my stomach."

The doctor said, "Get undressed and I'll examine you." During the examination the doctor asked, "What color are your stools?" "White," the patient replied.

The doctor was alarmed. "Nobody has white stools," he said to himself. "This person must really be sick. I'd better give him a very thorough workup." So he started to examine the patient again. As he did so, he said, "White stools! How long have you had them?"

The patient thought a moment. "Well, for about a year now. We redecorated the kitchen last year in white; so I painted the stools white to go with it."

There is a monastery where the monks are allowed to speak aloud on only one day of the year, and on that day only one monk is permitted to say anything.

One year on the appointed day, the monk whose turn it was to speak stood up and said, "I hate the mashed potatoes we have here. They're always lumpy."

Having spoken he sat down and lapsed into silence again. Another year passed by until the day for talking came once more. Another monk arose and said, "I like the mashed potatoes. I think they are delicious. In fact, I can hardly wait for the night when we have mashed potatoes."

Again silence for another year. Summer turned into autumn, and winter gave way to spring. Finally the day arrived when a third monk was allowed to speak.

"I want to transfer to another monastery," he said. "I can't stand this constant bickering."

An old lady had a parrot, and the only thing the parrot could say was, "Who is it?" One day the old lady went out shopping and the plumber came to her house. He rang the bell, and the parrot said, "Who is it?" "The plumber," the plumber replied. Again the parrot said, "Who is it?" The plumber replied, "It's the plumber, lady. Will you let me in." The parrot again responded with the only phrase it knew. The plumber answered with exasperation, but to no avail. After another dozen repeats of the same exchange, the plumber was so excited and upset he had a heart attack and dropped dead. When the old lady came home and saw the dead body lying outside her door, she ran over and cried, "Who is it?" "It's the plumber, lady!" the parrot replied.

A customer in a fruit store told the clerk he wanted to buy half a head of lettuce. The clerk told him they did not sell lettuce by halves—he must buy the whole head. The man insisted he didn't need the whole head. The clerk said, "Okay, I'll ask the boss."

The clerk went to the back of the store and said to the boss, "There is this jackass out front, and he wants to buy half a head of lettuce." At this point he turned and saw that the customer had followed him. He continued, thinking quickly, "This gentleman wants to by the other half." The boss said, "Okay, sell the two halves, and when you're finished I would like to see you."

So when the clerk finished with the customer he again went to the back to see the boss. The boss said, "That was very quick thinking. I like that, and I think you are what I will need. I'm going to open a fruit market in Montreal and would like you to run it. Are you interested?" "In Montreal?" the clerk responded. "No way! In Montreal all they have are prostitutes and hockey teams." "Oh really?" said the boss. "My wife is from Montreal." "Oh really?" the quick-thinking salesclerk answered. "What team did she play for?"

A patient was sitting in the dentist's chair.

"Good grief, you have the biggest cavity I've ever seen!" the dentist exclaimed as he examined the man. "The biggest cavity I've ever seen!"

The patient, very alarmed, snapped back at the dentist, "You didn't have to repeat it!"

"I didn't repeat it," replied the dentist. "That was an echo!"

A patient was making his first visit to the doctor.

"And who did you consult about your illness before you came to me?" asked the doctor.

"Only the druggest down at the corner," replied the patient.

The doctor could not hide his anger at the thought of medical advice being given by someone who wasn't a doctor. "And what sort of ridiculous advice did that fool give you?" he snarled.

"He told me to see you," replied the patient.

A man and a woman were in a quiet restaurant having an intimate dinner for two. As they were ordering cocktails, they suddenly heard a thunderous crash coming from the kitchen. Once the noise of breaking glass and dishes subsided, the woman hesitantly asked, "What was all that commotion about?" "That commotion, my dear lady," the waiter calmly replied, "was the sound of a job suddenly opening up."

They tell the story of Wilton Lackaye, who was scheduled to speak late on the program at a banquet at which all the speakers had been brutally long-winded.

Finally the chairman introduced Lackaye, saying, "Wilton Lackaye, the famous actor, will now give you his address."

Lackaye faced the haggard audience and said, "Mr. Chairman, Ladies and Gentlemen, my address is the Lamb's Club, New York."

He sat down to a tremendous ovation.

Mark Twain once asked a baggage handler at the railroad station in Washington, "Is that satchel strong enough to go in the baggage car?"

The baggage man lifted the grip high above his head and smashed it to the ground with all his might. "That," said he, "is what it will get in Philadelphia." He picked it up and bashed it against the side of the car four or five times. "That is what it will get in Chicago," he continued. He next threw it high in the air and, when it had landed, jumped on it vigorously. It split open and scattered its contents over the platform. "And that is what it will get in Sioux City," he said, according to Twain. "So if you are going any farther than Sioux City, you'd better take it in the Pullman with you."

CHAPTER 4

The Talk-Power Action Formula (The Building-Block Approach)

In *Anna Karenina,* Leo Tolstoy wrote, "All happy families resemble one another; every unhappy family is unhappy in its own fashion." Much the same could be said about good and bad speeches. There are as many ways for a speech to go wrong as there are speakers, but good speeches have certain characteristics in common.

All of us have listened to more than our share of bad speeches. We have heard speeches that were delivered so haltingly that we didn't care what was being said. We have heard speeches that were delivered smoothly, but which practically put us to sleep, as the speaker droned on endlessly and seemingly without point.

Some speeches are mere grocery lists of facts—too many facts to be absorbed by a listening audience. Some speeches ramble all over the place, so that it is impossible to tell where they are going. Others simply make no sense. The end of the speech seems to have no connection with the beginning.

Good speeches, on the other hand, whatever their subject and whatever their length, are fundamentally similar. A good speech is clear and consistent in its point of view, so that we know from beginning to end *why* it is being given. The facts and information included in the speech back up that point of view, telling us what we need to know without overloading our listening capacity. A good speech holds our attention and interest. And, finally, a good speech leaves us with the feeling that what we have heard is worth thinking or talking about further. We may not agree with the point of view the speaker has expressed, but if the speech has been a successful one, we will at least know why and how we disagree, and will feel the points the speaker has made are worth debating.

Even if the speaker has made us want to answer him back, he has nevertheless *engaged* us, caught our attention and made us think about what has been said. If we have been entertained, moved, or persuaded, so much the better. But even if we have been angered or dismayed, we must at least have been engaged.

The last two chapters have focused on techniques and exercises to help you overcome the physical discomfort and panic that afflict so many inexperienced public speakers. You have learned how to slow down, how to bring your instinctive bodily reactions under control. Now it is time for you actually to give a speech. In the next few chapters, you will learn step by step how to *organize* a speech that has a clear and consistent point of view, a speech that will engage your audience.

Most classes or books on public speaking emphasize that a speech should have a beginning, a middle and an end, or, put another way, that it should have an introduction, a body, and a conclusion. That's fine, as far as it goes. But in fact such advice is too vague. What often happens in actual practice is that the inexperienced speaker circles around for the first two or three minutes of his speech trying to find the beginning. By the time he stumbles onto it, the audience is already confused and restless, unsure about what the speaker is really trying to get across. The middle of the speech is likely to be muddled, jumping from point to point without any sense of logical development. And the end is often abrupt, as though the speaker had suddenly run into a brick wall.

As language theoretician Eric Lennenberg once noted, a sentence is somewhat analagous to a mosaic. "Put together stone after stone, yet the picture as a whole must have come into being in the artist's mind before he began to lay down the pieces." In the same sense a talk is a magnification of a sentence. One long major idea is put together section by section, yet the whole must be in the speaker's mind before he begins to lay down the pieces.

Even when we use the familiar beginning, middle, and end as a guideline for the organization of a talk, the result is far too often a rambling shapeless product. The reason for this is that beginning, middle, and end are simply too general as concepts. What is needed is a detailed understanding of exactly what belongs in the beginning, mid-

The Talk-Power Formula

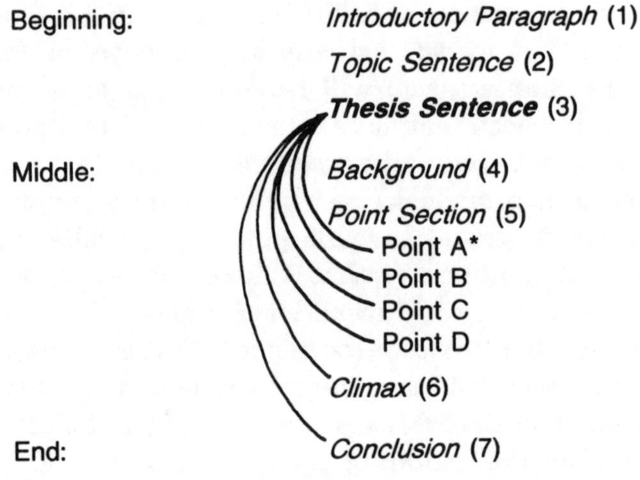

**Point* and *subheading* are synonymous.

dle, and end of a successful talk. The Talk-Power Formula will provide you that.

As you can see this formula divides the speech into seven distinct sections. Each one has a specific function, which will be discussed separately in the following chapters. A followup assignment based on each section will strengthen your learning experience.

For the inexperienced speaker, every new presentation becomes an unfamiliar risk in uncharted waters. By using a formula, each new presentation is approached with a familiar procedure, a systematic method for organization, and a repeatable technique.

With the formula, although each talk you do will be different from the one you did before, the structure will always follow the original model, giving you a feeling of security and confidence.

The formula can be used whether your talk is a five-minute presentation or a two-day seminar. How you handle each section will of course be determined by the amount of time you have to give your presentation.

In the next several chapters we will be going over the details of each section, so that you have a complete understanding of how each section is developed and how the entire talk is put together.

Visitors to my classes always remark on how enjoyable it is to listen to the speeches. There is a sense of fluency, not only in the delivery but, equally important, also in the material itself. The sense of vibrancy one gets is a natural byproduct of innovative methods for encouraging your natural and spontaneous thought processes to develop ideas. First, through brainstorming, which is explained in great detail in Chapter 8, and, second, through a unique method of developing and arranging your ideas around one central thesis.

In traditional classes, where overly long and tedious

speeches are the rule, the approach used is to join together all new ideas with transitional phrases called bridges. It has been my experience that this theory of transitional phrases acts as a mental straightjacket for both audience and speaker by too rigidly controlling the dynamic inner rhythms of a talk. It is *not necessary* to connect points to one another with a so-called logical bridge. Ideas need space; they need time to be breathed and osmosed into the consciousness of the audience.

When you create artificial transitions by welding ideas one to the other, more likely than not the result is a boring speech that never gets off the ground. **A simple pause of three seconds is all that is needed to effect a *real* transition,** and it is the *real* transitions that create the dynamic excitement of a well put together speech.

Using the Action Formula, you will be able to deliver speeches that are so logical and easy to follow that your tendency to block or forget important points or lose control will be reduced to a minimum. There will be little chance of panicking, because you will know exactly where you are going and will be confident that your audience is following the route you have taken.

Most speeches are unclear or unfocused because they do not develop a clear and consistent point of view. Many otherwise well-educated people simply have not been trained to translate their thinking into an oral message. They don't establish from the start of their talk a clear point of view that can be carried through consistently to the end. A speech is not a term paper or a fiscal report; you cannot use footnotes when you're talking to an audience.

Eminent historians, scientists, or philosophers often publish books based on a series of lectures they have given. "Based on," you will notice. Lectures that are published in book form are almost always revised by the author before publication. The original lectures were designed to be delivered aloud, in full awareness that a listening public cannot absorb information in the same way a reading public can. You can read as slowly as you want, but you must listen at the speed the speaker chooses for you.

The Action Formula will teach you how to write a speech and how to edit it yourself for a listening audience. Step by step, exercise by exercise, you will discover how to compose a speech that you can deliver comfortably and that your audience can readily absorb.

THE TALK-POWER WORD BUDGET

Let's look again at the sequence of the sections in the Talk-Power Action Formula.

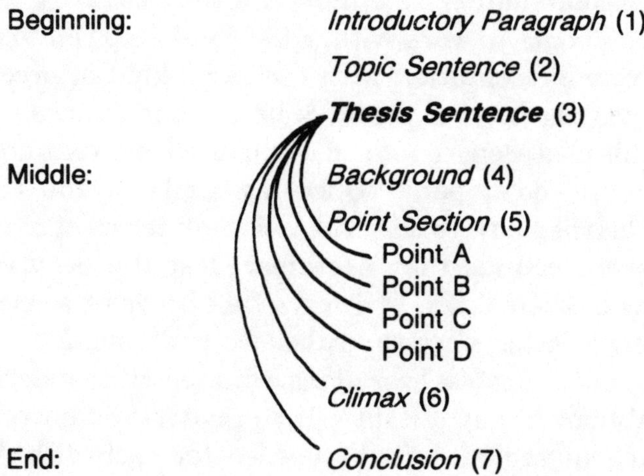

Each presentation usually has a time limitation. In the next step you will learn exactly how many minutes to spend on each section by referring to this time limitation.

Once you have decided how many minutes you can give

to each section you can determine how much material you need. This is how you do it:

There are about 150 words to each speaking minute. If you are given seven minutes to make a presentation, you will have to prepare about 1,050 words to fill the entire seven-minute period. This means that you will have to go back to the Action Formula and divide your seven minutes among your sections. A good time/word budget is:

- One minute for your introductory paragraph, topic sentence, and thesis sentence/150 words
- One minute for your background/150 words
- Four minutes for three or four points or subheadings/600 words
- One minute left for the climax and your summation (the conclusion)/150 words

This combination time limit and word count gives you a *word budget* to work with, which will help you to organize your presentation with the same kind of precision that you use in your business letters and memos.

If this idea seems a radical departure from your normal procedure, don't panic. Once my students and clients have learned how to edit themselves in terms of minutes and word counts, they are amazed at the beauty and clarity of their talks. Writing a talk becomes as easy as writing a letter, once the rules are understood.

No host or hostess ever plans a dinner without deciding exactly how many guests will be invited and how much of each ingredient will be needed for each dish. Your presentations deserve the same amount of planning.

To cover the points you want to get across in a given period of time when making a speech, you need a timetable. Here is a timetable that has been worked out for a seven-minute presentation:

Action Formula Word Budget

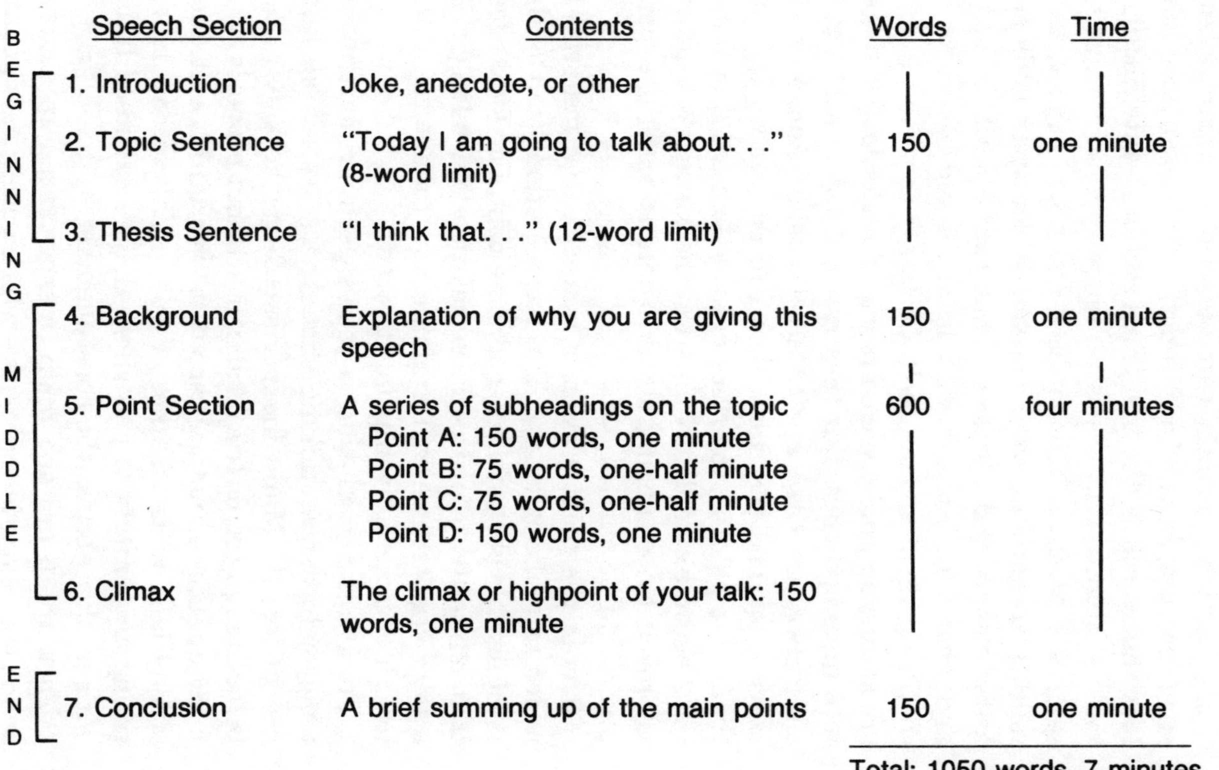

	Speech Section	Contents	Words	Time
BEGINNING	1. Introduction	Joke, anecdote, or other	150	one minute
	2. Topic Sentence	"Today I am going to talk about. . ." (8-word limit)		
	3. Thesis Sentence	"I think that. . ." (12-word limit)		
MIDDLE	4. Background	Explanation of why you are giving this speech	150	one minute
	5. Point Section	A series of subheadings on the topic Point A: 150 words, one minute Point B: 75 words, one-half minute Point C: 75 words, one-half minute Point D: 150 words, one minute	600	four minutes
	6. Climax	The climax or highpoint of your talk: 150 words, one minute		
END	7. Conclusion	A brief summing up of the main points	150	one minute

Total: 1050 words, 7 minutes

The Action Formula can be used to organize and structure a speech of any length. But, no matter how long the speech is, the first three sections—introduction, topic sentence, and thesis sentence—should always be restricted to about 150 words. If you take longer than a minute to get into your speech, to let your audience know clearly and concisely what your speech is about and what your point of view is, you stand in danger of confusing them and yourself. Certainly there are highly accomplished public speakers who do take longer to get into their speeches. But they can get away with it precisely because they are so accomplished and at ease. Having learned the rules, they can now afford to bend them. The point is, the rules must be learned first. They must become completely a part of the speaker's habitual approach to organizing a talk before successful experiments can be carried out.

It is in the point section of a speech that material is added to make it longer. The point section itself is the most flexible part of a speech. Some points may take less than a minute to cover; others may take much longer. In a later chapter, we will examine how to determine the length of time a given point deserves.

Finally, the conclusion to your speech, no matter how long you have been talking, should *never* exceed one minute in length. Many inexperienced speakers, as noted before, simply come to a dead halt, without properly summing up. Like a motorist about to overrun his exit, they simply jam on the brakes or veer wildly across lanes, trying desperately to get where they're supposed tc be, with no thought for the consequences.

Then there are the many inexperienced speakers—even some experienced ones—who commit the opposite mistake. In summing up their points, they repeat themselves in such detail that the audience begins to think the speech has started all over again.

A summary is by definition a very *brief* recapitulation. Book and film critics often summarize a three-hundred-page novel or a two-hour movie in a paragraph. **You do not need and should not take more than one minute to summarize a speech of any length.**

In the following chapters, I will be analyzing each section of the Action Formula step by step, using specific examples. You learn:

- How the introductory joke or anecdote leads into the Topic Sentence
- What other kinds of introductions there are
- What a topic sentence is
- How a thesis sentence differs from a topic sentence
- The importance of a background section explaining why you're giving the speech
- How you can decide which points are the most important when you've spent hours doing research for a ten-minute talk
- How you can identify your point of climax
- What you should leave out of your summary

And many other questions will be covered as well.

CHAPTER 5

How to Begin to Write a Speech (The Introductory Section)

In following the material below, first choose a topic for a speech you can be working on as we discuss each section of the Action Formula. Having a definite topic in mind will help you focus more concretely on the explanations and exercises presented.

CHOOSING THE TOPIC FOR YOUR SPEECH

Choose a topic that falls into one of the following categories:

1. A talk or speech you might be called on to make as part of your job
2. A talk or speech you might be asked to give before an organization or club you belong to
3. A talk or speech asking people to support a political candidate or lobbying organization
4. A talk or speech asking people to support a charity
5. An inspirational talk or speech
6. A talk or speech about something you particularly enjoy doing
7. A talk or speech about your favorite restaurant

For the first talk or speech, the topic I usually recommend in my classes is your favorite restaurant. That requires no research and is an excellent way to begin learning the principles of the Talk-Power system. However, if you are interested in any other topics in the indicated categories, by all means choose one that appeals to you.

The next step is to identify your *intention* in giving a speech about the topic you have chosen. In other words, **what is it you would like your audience to do after they hear your talk?**

As you will see in the chapters that follow, identifying your intention is crucial to delivering a successful speech.

Exercise Eight: Identifying Your Intention

Ideally, what would you like to have your audience do after hearing your talk or speech? (Check one of the following.)

Action Intentions

—— Invest with my company
—— Buy my product
—— Give my agency the account
—— Give my company the order
—— Act on my recommendation
—— Accept my report
—— Sign a petition
—— Vote for my program or idea
—— Vote for my candidate
—— Unite behind a particular action by forming a committee
—— Protest with a particular action
—— Respond generously with a commitment of time/money
—— Be inspired

—— Have a sense of sharing
—— Try something new
—— Want to know me better
—— Write a letter
—— Learn how to do a procedure
—— Understand an idea
—— Share my experience
—— Feel unified
—— Feel welcomed

Notice that your intention is always stated with an action verb. Your ability to articulate your intention that way will help you project your message with great energy and belief. A talk or speech is an important opportunity for you to charge your audience with the kind of confidence and enthusiasm that motivates them to move on your recommendations. Your vision of exactly what it is that you would like them to do is essential to this process. Without this articulated vision, you run the risk of an energy-inhibited presentation.

No matter what your presentational style, be it dynamic, extroverted, laid back, restrained, formal, or casual, in the back of your mind you must always have a very clear picture of what it is that you want your audience to *do* after they have heard your talk. Don't think about what the effect upon them will be, but about what it is that you would like them to *do,* or in the case of the inspirational talk, to feel.

Exercise Nine: Your Intention

Now, take a 5 × 8 card and write on it the category of talk or speech you intend to give, as listed on the previous page. For example, you may have chosen a talk or speech to give before a club or organization you belong to. If so, your intention in giving that speech might be any of the following action directives:

- Take my recommendation and act on it.
- Vote for my program or idea.
- Side with me.
- Vote for my candidate.
- Give money.
- Unite behind a particular action by forming a committee.
- Be inspired.
- Want to know me better.

On the 5 × 8 card, write down the intention you have checked. Then write out in ten words or less the topic you intend to speak on.

Keep your 5 × 8 card handy as you read the next section. With your topic and intention clearly in mind, let's see how you construct a speech using the Action Formula.

The Talk-Power Formula

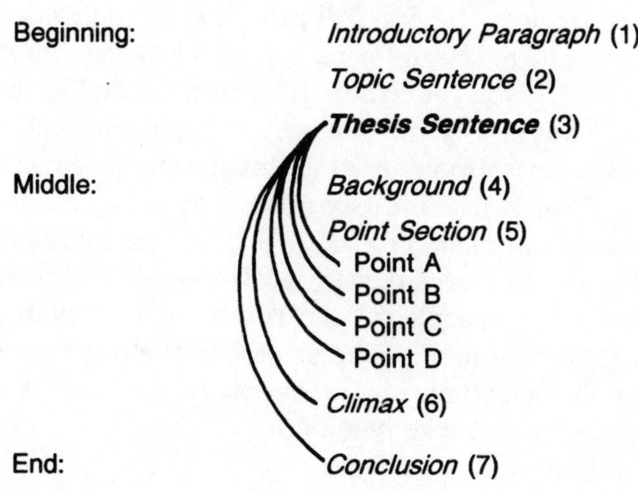

THE INTRODUCTORY SECTION

The beginning of your speech, the introductory section, will have three parts:

1. A joke or anecdote
2. A topic sentence
3. A thesis sentence

Each of these three parts has a particular purpose.

Why, you may ask, begin with a joke or anecdote? Why not get right to the point?

The fact is that when you first stand up to speak, the audience is very busy looking at you, taking you in, observing and making mental notes about your age, sex, color, height, weight, clothes, attractiveness, and even your resemblance to other people. The audience members are arriving at a general impression of your voice, speech, and manner—indeed, of your total image.

All of this happens in the first thirty to sixty seconds of your appearance before the group. During these moments the audience is very involved in this unconscious process, too busy to give full attention to the content of your speech, to the information you have so carefully researched. If you get right to the point, the audience may miss it. That is why the best way to begin your talk is to present a very simple, easy to understand story or joke.

In addition, a joke is an excellent way to begin a speech because of the mood of good-will that usually accompanies humor. In a recent study at Texas A&M University on persuading people to contribute small amounts of money, the telling of a joke as part of the pitch resulted in contributions that were on average more than twice as large as when no joke was told.

The kind of joke that produces the most desirable effect is one that tells a very concrete story, follows a logical chain of events that is easy to understand, and *relates to the subject of the talk that will follow.*

The joke or story should not be shorter than seventy-five words or longer than 150 words, and it should have a punch line or strong, clearly conclusive last line.

An introductory joke doesn't have to be so funny that it makes audience members split their sides with laughter. Your object isn't to launch a career as a standup comic. Neither is your purpose to capture, conquer, overwhelm, or hypnotize your audience. Your purpose is simply to initiate a give-and-take flow between yourself and your audience while its members are in the process of adjusting to your presence. A mildly amusing anecdote that doesn't put too much pressure on the audience will be fine, giving you a chance to begin your presentation in an easy and friendly manner.

Other Kinds of Introductions

If you feel truly uncomfortable with the idea of beginning your speech with a joke, or if a joke doesn't seem appropriate to the occasion, there are other kinds of introductions you can use. For instance, you might well prefer to use a different approach for a business presentation. Business presentations may differ from other public speaking situations in several ways. You may be speaking to a small group consisting of people who know one another to some degree. There may be no need to set those who are listening to you at ease. Or you may feel that a joke would seem frivolous and put you in a bad light.

In such situations it is perfectly appropriate and effective to begin your talk with your *topic sentence.* For example: "The purpose of my report is to present the final draft of the XYZ proposal." Then you would follow immediately with your *thesis sentence:* "I believe that this version is a great improvement over other approaches we have considered."

In most speaking situations, however, including business addresses before large groups, some kind of introduction should precede the topic sentence. A simple and effective way to begin is to make use of a technique I devised for my students and clients. I call it the East-West Method. The East-West introduction provides the audience with four simple statements of fact about *one* subject. Here are a few examples:

Some people use a taxi only when they are late.
Some people use a taxi every day.
Others may use a cab for that special date.
Still others never ride in a cab because the ticking of the meter makes them nervous.
Topic sentence: Today I am going to talk about taxi cabs.

Some secretaries are expected to make coffee for the boss.
Others are asked to do personal shopping.
Some secretaries have to water the plants in the office.
I even know of a secretary who was asked to help serve at a buffet given by her boss.
Topic sentence: Today I am going to talk about secretaries.

The price of flowers is rising sky high.
On Lexington Avenue, roses sell for $1.50 apiece.
On Columbus Avenue, gardenias are $25.00 a dozen.
Even on Wall Street, a bunch of daisies costs $3.00.
Topic sentence: Today I am going to talk about making your own flowers.

The East-West introduction is a series of four basic factual statements about one subject. There should be no defense, explanation, or elaboration. All of that comes later in the speech, during the point section.

A speech can also be introduced by a single statement or question, but it must be strong enough to grab the audience's immediate attention. You can, for instance, begin with a *shocking statement.*

> By late 1923 prices in Germany had increased 726 million times over what they had been five years earlier in 1918.
> *Topic sentence:* Today I am going to talk about inflation.

> More people are seriously injured in their own homes than anywhere else.
> *Topic sentence:* Today I am going to talk about making your home a safer place to live.

Another form of one-sentence introduction is the *rhetorical question.* This kind of introduction works in the same manner as the shocking statement. By phrasing the information as a question that does not have to be answered, you can often catch the audience's attention even more quickly.

> Did you know that Parker Brothers prints about the same amount of money annually for Monopoly® sets as the United States Treasury prints for genuine use?
> *Topic sentence:* Today I am going to talk about the big business of games.

Using a quotation—from a famous person, from a newspaper article or editorial, or even a well-known line from a movie or play—can make for a snappy beginning to a speech. In general, the shorter the quotation, the better. If you are using a quotation from a newspaper or magazine, avoid complex statements that include too many facts, explanations, or qualifying remarks. If the quotation is too long, too abstract, or too complicated, your audience will be confused before you even get to your own topic sentence.

> Ann Landers once said, "Television has proved that people will look at anything rather than each other."
> *Topic sentence:* Today I am going to discuss the effect of television on family relationships.
>
> Former Senator Eugene McCarthy once said, "Being in politics is like being a football coach. You have to be smart enough to understand the game and dumb enough to think it's important."
> *Topic sentence:* Today I want to discuss why Americans are so disillusioned with politics.
>
> In a recent *Newsweek* column, Jane Bryant Quinn wrote, "Any teenager can tell you that it is smart to borrow and dumb to save. The way to get ahead is to stay in debt, write off the interest payments on your tax return, and repay your loans in cheaper dollars."
> *Topic sentence:* Today I want to talk about teaching teenagers the value of money.

Finally, a verse from a poem is sometimes useful as an introduction to a speech. You have to be careful with poetry, though. The verse you choose shouldn't be too abstract or difficult in its construction. Much modern poetry, for instance, reads more easily on the page than it does aloud. It is best to choose a well-known passage that a majority of your audience is likely to be at least somewhat familiar with. Because poetry often deals with universal ideas, a single quotation can be used to introduce many different topics, so if you're stuck for an introductory remark, you may well find some appropriate lines by glancing through an anthology of poetry.

Whatever form of introductory remark you choose—joke, humorous anecdote, the East-West method, shocking statement, rhetorical question or quotation—remember that it should not exceed 150 words, no matter how long your speech is to be.

A Pause after Your Introduction

After the last words of your introductory remark you will need a brief pause or a rest period. This is done by *not* speaking and silently counting to five. This pause allows you to let go of some tension and allows for a brief transition period before you go on to the next idea. In using the Talk-Power Action Formula, you will find that a rest period is called for after each section is completed. My students have found that the best way to remember to pause is to write in large letters at the end of each section REST PERIOD—COUNT TO FIVE.

Once you've finished your introduction, your audience should be ready to listen. You will have given everyone the few moments needed to take you in and settle down.

Exercise Ten: Writing an Introduction

1. Take out the 5 × 8 card on which you wrote your intention and topic in Exercise Nine.
2. Select one type of introduction that would be appropriate to the topic you have already selected.
3. Write out your introduction on one or more 5 × 8

cards, skipping every other line so that you can read the material easily if necessary.

4. Be sure to write the words REST PERIOD—COUNT TO FIVE after the last word. Keep this card at hand. You will be needing it again shortly.

Now you are ready to move on to the next chapter, which deals with the topic and thesis sentences. These elements will complete the beginning section of your speech.

CHAPTER 6

Getting Your Message Across (The Topic Sentence and Thesis Sentence)

The Talk-Power Formula

Beginning:	*Introductory Paragraph* (1)
	Topic Sentence (2)
	Thesis Sentence (3)
Middle:	*Background* (4)
	Point Section (5) Point A Point B Point C Point D
	Climax (6)
End:	*Conclusion* (7)

THE TOPIC SENTENCE (2)

The topic sentence always follows the last line of your joke. **The purpose of the topic sentence is to point you and your audience in the *general direction* your talk is headed.**

To give you a picture of how a topic sentence follows your introductory remark, here is an *example:*

> A truck driver was asked about the food at a certain truck stop along his busy route. "The food there is terrible," he said. "The mashed potatoes are watery, the green beans are tasteless, the roast beef is tough, the pie crust is limp and leathery, and the coffee tastes like dishwater. But worst of all, they serve such small portions."
>
> *(Pause)*
>
> *Topic sentence:* Today I am going to talk about choosing a good restaurant.

The topic sentence should be like the title of a book: *short.* It is simply a title, or headline, without explanations. Keeping the topic sentence as short as possible will discourage any tendency you have to wander, drift, or lose control. It is a simple *direction sign*—functioning somewhat like a street sign.

Let's look at some examples of right and wrong topic sentences.

Right

- Today I am going to talk about the new budget.
- Today I am going to talk about the subway situation.

- Today I am going to describe some new procedures in the department.

- Today I am going to talk about our annual fund drive.

Wrong

- Today I am going to talk about a subject which is not going to be very popular here, because of all the reasons that were outlined in Mr. Jones' annual report last Thursday —and you all must know what I mean by now, and I do mean the new budget.

- Today I am going to talk about the most deplorable situation that any city can possibly imagine in the grimmest of dreams, because there has simply got to be some sort of a solution to the dilemma of our subways.

- As you all know, there have been some new procedures that many people feel are rather complicated and also costly, as they take a considerable amount of paperwork, but I will try to explain them to you so that there will be a minimum of unfortunate error.

- Today I am going to talk about our annual fund drive in the hope that all of you will pitch in and lend a hand and be as generous as you possibly can.

The *wrong* topic sentences are all too long, too complicated, and give too much information. Length, complexity, and excess information hinder clear communication with a listening audience. A listening audience cannot turn back the page if it has missed something. A listening audience has to absorb what you say as you say it; this is especially crucial at the beginning of your talk. A topic sentence is like a headline, immediately telegraphing the subject of what follows for quick comprehension.

Topic Sentences from Jokes

Your topic sentence, as previously noted, should have some relevance to the story or joke you have told. But that does not mean you have to search endlessly for the perfect joke. Any brief joke or story can be used to introduce a wide variety of topics, as the following example illustrates:

> A young English author was due to deliver the first speech of his American lecture tour. "I'm such a miserable speaker," he confessed to his American agent, "that I know they'll all walk out on me before I finish." "Nonsense!" retorted the agent. "You are an excellent speaker and will keep the audience glued to their seats." "Oh, I say," cried the author, "that is a wonderful idea! But do we dare?"

Possible Topic Sentences

Today I am going to talk about public speaking.

Today I am going to talk about nervousness.

The subject of my talk is lecture tours.

Tonight I am going to talk about English authors.

I am here to tell you about agents and authors.

It is not only easy to pull topic sentences out from jokes or anecdotes, it is fun. Try it for yourself.

Exercise Eleven: Writing Topic Sentences

The following exercise has two purposes. First, it will give you a chance to practice writing out short, clear topic sentences. Second, it will help you understand the relationship between the introductory joke or anecdote and the topic sentence that follows.

Read the joke below, and then try to find four topic sentences that relate to it. Write out each topic sentence on a 5 × 8 card.

Two men working side by side in the War Production Board in Washington never spoke, but each watched the other. One man quit work daily at four o'clock, while the other always worked till six or later. Finally the harder worker approached the other. "I beg your pardon," he said. "Do you mind telling me how you clean up all your work every day at four o'clock?"

"Not at all, when I come to a tough piece of detail, I mark it: *Refer to Commander Smith.* I figure that in an outfit as large as this there is sure to be a Commander Smith, and I must be right. None of those papers come back to me."

"Brother," said the hard worker, removing his coat, "prepare for action—I am Commander Smith."

Possible Topic Sentences

Today I am going to talk about ____________________

The subject of my talk is ____________________

Tonight I am going to talk about ____________________

I am here to tell you about ____________________

Here are a few possible topic sentences you might have found in this little story.

Today I am going to talk about office organization.

The subject of my talk is bureaucracy.

Tonight I am going to talk about worker productivity.

I am here to tell you about a computerized filing system.

There are at least a dozen other possible topic sentences that can be derived from this one story. Do not worry if none of yours is similar to the examples above. In fact, you can play a game with yourself—try to find as many topic sentences as possible. But *keep them short.*

The Talk-Power Formula

Beginning:	*Introductory Paragraph* (1)
	Topic Sentence (2)
	Thesis Sentence (3)
Middle:	*Background* (4)
	Point Section (5) Point A Point B Point C Point D
	Climax (6)
End:	*Conclusion* (7)

THE THESIS SENTENCE (3)

Let's take a different joke, leading to a different topic sentence, and examine the purpose of the *thesis sentence,* which comprises the third part of the beginning of your speech.

> An anonymous New York taxpayer sent a letter to the State Comptroller's Office in Albany saying that he had cheated on his income tax ten years ago and had not been able to get a

good night's sleep since. He enclosed $25 and added: "If I still can't sleep, I will send the balance."

(Pause)

Topic sentence: Today I am going to talk about income tax.

(Pause)

Thesis sentence: I think that the proposed federal income tax cuts are not in the best interests of the country.

Your thesis sentence is the most important sentence in your talk. It is the one idea you would like your audience to hear and remember clearly. It is your main point of view, the spine or central pillar of your presentation.

The reason it is so important is that the thesis sentence is your instrument for building *drive* into your talk. This sentence helps you maintain the interest, motivation, and involvement of your audience.

In a good presentation, all the material, no matter how diverse and broad, is organized and designed around your one thesis sentence.

It is important you note the word *one* here. Time and time again clients and students who have taken public speaking courses at universities or elsewhere tell me they have been taught that you can have more than one thesis to a speech.

Let us put an end to this idea once and for all. The false belief that a speech can have more than one thesis causes much of the anxiety people have when writing speeches. In addition, it invariably results in a confused talk. No talk or presentation that is delivered in one sitting can have more than one thesis. If you have heard a speech with two main theses, you have heard not one speech, but two.

A thesis is a powerful idea that moves in one direction. It is like a spine attached to one pair of legs. If you had two spines with two different sets of legs, the movement would be in two different directions and the results chaotic. Confusion and anxiety would be inevitable. Use the Talk-Power model, with one thesis, and you will discover that your ability to control and develop your point of view is greatly facilitated.

The placement of this thesis sentence is crucial to the success of your talk. The thesis sentence must *always* appear in the first section of your talk, because:

- It gives the audience a path to travel.
- If you tell the audience where you are going, they will help you get there.
- A sense of security develops in the audience when they have a firm, clear grasp of what it is you mean to say and what it is you wish them to do.
- There is much greater willingness to trust a person who declares his intentions early on in the game.
- It becomes the frame of reference for all the other remarks you make. As a result, there can be little opportunity for misunderstanding.

The thesis sentence is the instrument that communicates both the speaker's *enthusiasm* for and *commitment* to his point of view. It provides an opportunity to charge the room with energy and life simply because the speaker takes the risk of publicly revealing personal convictions. This is why the thesis statement should be preceded by one of the following phrases:

- "I think . . ."
- "I believe . . ."

- "I feel . . ."
- "I am committed to the idea that . . ."
- "I am of the opinion that . . ."

Note this example:

> A tourist on the road in Nova Scotia saw an Acadian lying with his ear to the ground. He walked over to him and heard the Acadian muttering, "Cadillac convertible, yellow fancy hub caps, man driving, large suitcase beside him, license plate."
>
> The tourist was astounded. "Do you mean that you can tell all that just by listening with your ear to the ground?"
>
> "Ear to the ground, nothing!" said the Acadian. "That car ran me down."
>
> *Topic sentence:* Tonight I am going to talk about my motor trip through Nova Scotia.
>
> *Thesis sentence:* I think Nova Scotia is a unique and wonderful place to visit.

By using direct, strongly personal phrases to present your central theme, you infuse your talk with a powerful human component. That human component will in turn intensify your audience's interest and raise its level of response.

To many people saying "I feel" or "I think" seems a sign of hesitancy. They prefer to "let the facts speak for themselves," relying on charts or graphs or statistics. They feel that to venture a personal opinion is to risk undermining their credibility. But a personal statement is a powerful instrument of persuasion. When a personal statement is followed by well-researched facts backing up the expressed point of view, the talk as a whole becomes stronger, not weaker.

Even in a corporate presentation, an expression of personal faith in a policy or action helps to communicate the strength of the message. If you have any doubts about that, consider the success of the advertising campaigns for Perdue chickens or Eastern Airlines, in which Frank Perdue and Frank Borman speak in the first person to sell their company's products or services.

Let's see how the opening joke, the topic sentence, and the thesis sentence relate to one another. Here are a joke and a topic sentence, with five different possibilities for a thesis sentence. (Remember there is only one thesis to a speech.)

> A shy young man came into the office of a go-getter sales manager, timidly approached the desk, and mumbled, "You don't want to buy any insurance, do you?"
>
> "No!" was the brusque reply.
>
> "I was afraid not," said the embarrassed chap, starting to back toward the door.
>
> "Wait a minute!" exclaimed the sales manager. "I've dealt with salesmen all my life, and you're the worst I've ever seen. You have to inspire confidence, and to do that you've got to have it yourself. Just to give you the confidence that can make a sale, I'll sign for a $10,000 policy."
>
> After signing the application, the sales manager said, "What you have to do is learn some good techniques and use them."
>
> "Oh, but I have," returned the salesman. "I have an approach for almost every type of businessman. The one I just used was my standard approach for sales managers."

Topic sentence: Today I am going to talk about selling.

Thesis possibilities:

- I believe that a successful selling technique is based on a variety of approaches.

- I think even the most experienced salesman can still learn a new approach.
- I am committed to the idea that it takes more than confidence to make a good salesman.
- I feel very strongly that the young salesman should be taken more seriously by the older competitor.
- I am of the opinion that with the right approach even the most difficult customer can be sold.

As you can see, each one of these thesis sentences takes a specific focus that differs from the other four. Using each one of these sentences as a guideline, you would ultimately have five quite different speeches.

Good Thesis Sentences

Let us briefly analyze each one of these thesis sentences in terms of the main focal points:

1. "I believe that a successful selling technique is based on a variety of approaches."

The speaker will be talking about the various selling techniques that lead to successful selling. This is probably a training talk.

2. "I think even the most experienced salesman can still learn a new approach."

The speaker will be focusing on *new* approaches, attempting to motivate more experienced salesmen to try new and different selling techniques, asking them not to rely so much on past performance.

3. "I am committed to the idea that it takes more than confidence to make a good salesman."

The speaker will talk about a variety of components—psychological, physical, etc.—required in order for one to become a good salesman. This talk would emphasize the personal qualifications necessary in a good salesman rather than sales techniques. This could be a recruitment talk.

4. "I feel very strongly that the young salesman should be taken more seriously by the older competitor."

The speaker will try to raise the consciousness of the more seasoned salesman to the real competitive loss he will experience if he does not pay more attention to the techniques, general enthusiasm, and energy of the new and younger sales competition.

5. "I am of the opinion that with the right approach even the most difficult customer can be sold."

Here we have the speaker focusing in on the difficult customer. This talk will concern itself with analyzing problems involved in selling to the difficult customer and reviewing methods that have proven successful in this area.

Bad Thesis Sentences

Here are several thesis sentences that incorporate a common element of fault:

1. "I believe that successful selling techniques are based on a variety of approaches, because it has been proven time and time again that you can't keep relying on the same old strategies for every single type of customer."

This was fine until we got to the *because*. **Never have *because* in your thesis.** Don't explain!

2. "I believe that the most experienced salesman can still learn a new approach, and especially in view of present statistics showing that our competitors are running

away with the market, it would be wise to expand our repertoire of techniques."

This was fine until we got to the words *and especially.* **Never qualify a thesis.**

3. "It seems to me it might be better if even very experienced salesmen made the effort to try new techniques."

This is a very tentative half-hearted approach. ("It *seems* to me it *might be* better. . . .) This is a weak, unsure, hesitant way to take a position. It is definitely no way to express a thesis sentence.

4. "I think that the problem of the difficult customer must be dealt with on an individual basis, insofar as it has been our experience that difficult customers, when satisfied with our service and attention, can become our most desirable clients."

This was strong and fine until it got to *insofar.* After that word, the impact and strength of the preceding statement was diminished by the addition of another idea.

Idea A: "Difficult customers must be dealt with on an individual basis."
Idea B: "Difficult customers can become our most desirable clients."

Idea B should certainly be addressed, but it should not be included in the main thesis sentence.

To sum up, a thesis sentence should be a brief declarative statement that communicates to the audience your point of view on the topic you are speaking about.

A thesis sentence should *not:*

- Explain
- Defend
- Elaborate on the idea

- Give examples
- Develop itself in any way
- Have any words that are not absolutely necessary to conveying the meaning of what you have to say

Later in the speech you will be explaining, defending, elaborating, and giving examples. None of that takes place in the thesis sentence. The audience needs to understand what your point of view is before you begin to explain or defend. A simple statement achieves that best.

Exercise Twelve: Beginning Your Own Speech

1. Look at the 5 × 8 cards you made out at the end of the previous chapter. There you wrote down the category of speech you want to give, your intention in giving the speech, and the introductory joke or other selection that you have decided to use.

2. Take a fresh 5 × 8 card. On the first line, write out your *topic sentence.* Refer back to the description of the topic you wrote down at the end of the previous chapter. Can you make it shorter, more concise, more to the point? Probably you can.

3. Skip a few lines and then write out a *thesis sentence* for your speech, observing the rules set forth in this chapter. Read the thesis sentence over. Is your thesis stated in such a way that it will really help you accomplish your intention? If not, work on it some more. Look back to the examples we presented a few pages back.

An excellent way to evaluate your thesis sentence is to ask, "Can this thesis be a headline in a newspaper?" For instance, in my class I usually hold up a card with a thesis sentence and say, "Mr. Jones states that *as a result of high interest rates, the real estate market is suffering a severe loss.*" Of course you can see immediately that this thesis statement (in italics) is much too long to be a headline. If instead we say, "Mr. Jones states that *high interest rates are hurting the real estate market,"* we have essentially the same idea but with fewer words.

If at this point you have difficulty in coming up with a thesis sentence, select a different topic to speak on. You may tell yourself you're having trouble because your material is so rich or complex. But more likely, the problem is that you have not yet arrived at a point of view about your material. And in order to communicate successfully with an audience, you must have a point of view, a thesis.

If you haven't developed a point of view on a subject but have to give a speech on it nevertheless, you have two choices. You can rethink your position, trying once again to define your point of view. Or right at the start you can tell the audience that you really do not have a point of view. Unless you tell them you have not reached a decision concerning your point of view, the audience will spend their entire time trying to figure out what you are talking about and where you are going. However, rarely is a subject so complex or the choices so difficult that you just want to present your audience with alternatives to think about. Moreover, speeches without a clear perspective usually are not very interesting. The absence of a point of view may be appropriate to an encyclopedia; it is not appropriate to an oral presentation. It is almost always better to choose a different topic on which you do have a definite point of view.

Exercise Thirteen: Rehearsal

You are now ready to begin practicing the beginning of your speech. You will have three cards: the first with a joke, the second with a topic sentence, and the third with a thesis sentence written on it.

Once again, set up your rehearsal space as described in Exercise Seven in Chapter 3. Make sure you have your cards with you. Follow the full sequence of steps below.

1. Sit in your chair; center yourself.
2. With your cards in your lap, shake your hands vigorously (twenty shakes).
3. Concentrate on the tingling in your fingertips.
4. Take your cards in your hand.
5. *Very slowly* pull yourself up to your feet.
6. Stand in place and balance your weight evenly on both feet.
7. Step forward on your right foot, then your left foot; stop on both feet; concentrate on your fingertips. Do this until you have walked up to the front of your imaginary audience.
8. Slowly turn to face your imaginary audience, keeping your arms at your sides.
9. Run through your checklist.

Checklist

My head feels . . .
My eyes are . . .
My mouth is . . .
My shoulders are . . .
My neck is . . .
My chest feels . . .
My heart is . . .
My arms are . . .
My stomach is . . .
My hands feel . . .
My legs feel . . .
My knees are . . .
The bottom of my feet are . . .

10. Now begin to speak, trying not to look at your cards as you tell your joke or introductory anecdote.

11. Pause.

12. Give your topic sentence. Pause.

13. Give your thesis sentence. Pause again.

14. Walk back to your seat, and sit quietly for ten gentle breaths.

15. Now immediately repeat this sequence until ten minutes have gone by. (Use a kitchen timer.)

Progress Report

Date	Time	Strong spot	Weak spot	Comment	Calm–Nervous (1–10)

CHAPTER 7

How to Get People to Care (The Background Section)

Mr. Taylor is an account executive who is often asked to make presentations before clients. Always well prepared, Mr. Taylor feels quite comfortable about standing in front of people and presenting a talk. Yet his performance often leaves those who hear him with the sense that he is rather cold.

Everyone in the office knows that Taylor is in actuality a witty, warm, and generous person, a man with whom people feel very comfortable in a one-to-one meeting or a small group. Yet when he gets up to speak, he seems to lose the warmth of his personality and becomes a rather chilly presenter of facts.

What is the problem here? He doesn't experience the fears or mental lapses that affect so many inexperienced public speakers. He's very professional and businesslike —too businesslike.

The problem is that Mr. Taylor never refers to himself in any way. When making a presentation, he resolutely avoids the word *I*. He builds his arguments solely on facts and figures, avoiding any personal references, recommendations, or indications of preference.

The result is that Mr. Taylor the individual is simply not present. By avoiding all personal references, he loses the opportunity to communicate the warmth of his personality to the audience.

How can Mr. Taylor get across that warmth, and become more human to his audiences, without becoming inappropriately personal and without losing his professional credibility?

The answer lies in making proper use of the fourth section of the Action Formula: the *background* section.

The Talk-Power Formula

Beginning:	*Introductory Paragraph* (1)
	Topic Sentence (2)
	Thesis Sentence (3)
Middle:	*Background* (4)
	Point Section (5) Point A Point B Point C Point D
	Climax (6)
End:	*Conclusion* (7)

DEVELOPING THE BACKGROUND (4)

The background follows directly after your thesis sentence. It should contain a maximum of 150 words and a minimum of 75 words, no matter how long your speech will be. The purpose of the background is to make a personal connection between you and your audience.

The background answers the following question: **How did you or your company become interested in the topic of the speech?** Not the thesis, but the topic. The background is *not* a sales pitch. It is a *story* that explains to the audience why you want to talk about a given topic. It should have a minimum of abstractions, theories, statistics, or numbers. The background is first and foremost about you and your connection to your topic.

Why, you may be asking, should the audience want to know about you?

The answer is simple. People are interested in other people. They are especially interested in the personal life of those in the limelight, leaders and authority figures. Merely standing up to give a talk puts you in the limelight, makes you a leader. People—your audience—will want to know something about you.

What you tell your audience about yourself and your interest in the topic of your speech can be quite trivial. Because you are in the limelight, even trivial information becomes interesting. If you doubt that, consider the endless curiosity of the press about what politicians or movie stars eat for lunch. It doesn't really matter whether a person prefers cottage cheese with ketchup or eggs benedict; the public likes to know such things. These kinds of details humanize people in the limelight, makes them more real. Being more real makes your speech more interesting.

If you humanize yourself when making a speech, your audience will become more interested in what you are going to say about your topic, more receptive to your thesis, and more relaxed.

Just as your entrance remark (the joke or anecdote you begin with) allows the audience time to adjust to your physical and vocal presence, so the background gives the audience *a chance to know you* a little. It gives them a chance to begin to identify with you. Without that kind of identification, your audience will be less receptive to the facts and figures you present in the main body of your speech.

Let's look at the background remarks made by one of my students, a young woman delivering a speech about computers. After her introductory anecdote she identified her subject with her *topic sentence.* "Today I am going to talk about computers." She paused and then followed with her *thesis sentence:* "I think computers will become an essential part of our everyday lives in the eighties." After another moment of pause she presented the *background.*

> I first became interested in computers twelve years ago. At that time I was waiting for a job opportunity to open up at Rutgers University. While I was waiting, they offered me a temporary position at the computer center. Having nothing else to do, I decided to try it. The computers were not quite as powerful or functional as they are today, but they were massive and sophisticated and certainly much bigger than anything I had ever seen. All I had ever been exposed to was an electronic adding machine. I was fascinated with the computers.
>
> When the other job fell through, the data systems manager offered me a job at the computer center. He volunteered to train me. I jumped at the opportunity.
>
> Since that time I've been an application programer, a business programer, a program manager, and, most recently, a consultant. My fascination with computers has never ended.

In less than one minute, this young woman humanized herself and made clear her personal connection to the subject, computers. She revealed herself to her audience with a very simple story and made it easier for them to settle back and listen to what she had to say about her subject. Now she could go on to support her thesis, persuading her audience that computers will become an essential part of our everyday lives in the eighties.

There are some people, however, who find it almost impossible to talk about themselves in front of other people for more than a sentence or two. If you ask them questions, you can draw them out, but when left on their own to write a background section to their speeches, they cannot do it. For those people, I have developed a model for writing out a personal history. By using this model, answering each question in it simply and directly, you can put together a background that will enable you to tell an audience easily and fluently about your interest in the topic you are speaking on.

Model for the Background

If you feel that one of your problems is your inability to stick to a story line, here is a model for the background section. Use it as a guide for the background.

When did you first become involved or interested in the *topic* of your talk?

I became interested in (one or two sentences at most) ______

______

______

______

How did you hear about it? (one or two sentences at most) ______

______

______

How did you feel about it or what did you think about it at the time?

____

____

So *what* did you do? (one or two sentences)

____

____

Who else was involved? (one or two sentences)

____

____

What happened as a result? (Give three things if you can.)

1. (one sentence)
2. (one sentence)
3. (one sentence)

Bring us up to *the present* time.

Today I (one or two sentences at most)

____

____

In some cases, a truly personal history may be inappropriate. There are some circumstances in which an individual is speaking for his company and use of a first person narrative is awkward. But if you are the president of the company or were directly involved in formulating the policies or developing the product you are going to talk about, the personal background should be used. If you are simply a spokesperson reporting your company's corporate position on a particular topic, a less personal tone may be necessary.

That does not mean, however, that the background section of the talk should be skipped. Your audience will want to know why your company, which you personify, is interested in the topic. You can still personalize your background remarks to some extent by referring to "my company" rather than always using its full corporate name.

Here is a model for developing a corporate history to use in your speech.

Model for Corporate/Agency History

When did your company first become interested in or connected with this issue, product, new system, political problem, etc.? (one sentence)

____

____

How did your company hear about it or become connected with it? (one sentence)

____

____

What was the company's *point of view* or policy about such matters at that time? (one sentence)

____

____

What action did your company take? (one or two sentences)

____

____

____

What *other* companies or agencies were contacted? (one sentence)

____

____

What happened as a result? (Give three things if you can.)

1. (one sentence)
2. (one sentence)
3. (one sentence)

What is *the present* status of the issue or the company's point of view? (one sentence)

____

____

Model for a Wholly Impersonal Background

In the event that you under no circumstances can or wish to refer to yourself or your corporation and absolutely insist upon referring only to the topic you are discussing, here is a third model to follow. (Usually this form is used in a committee report or a school presentation.)

"The history of ______________ dates back to __________________.

"Originally (one sentence) ____."

Now *give three interesting facts* about the topic. (one sentence each)

1. ____
2. ____
3. ____

"As time went by . . . [*Give three things that happened.*]

____

____

____

____

What happened as a result? (three sentences)

"As a result ______________________________

____

____

Bring us up to *the present* time. (three sentences) ___

____

____

(Total: 150 words)

THE SKILL OF SELF-EDITING

Strive for *brevity* in filling out whichever model you employ. Many of my students or clients have told me that a major problem they encountered in writing a speech was their inability to edit themselves. In preparing a speech that was supposed to last just ten minutes, they would invariably amass reams of material—page after page of research data, evidence, and general information. Then when they got up to give the actual speech, they found themselves overwhelmed by their own material.

As one client, an attorney, put it, "When I get up to speak I find myself going on and on about one idea I want to get across, and then I suddenly realize that I'm not going to have time to say all the things I need to include.

It makes me panicky. It's like a dream I sometimes have. In this dream, I go into my office and all of my filing cabinets have been turned upside down and emptied out on the floor. I need certain documents quickly, to prepare a summation for a jury, and I don't know where anything is. I feel rushed and helpless; I don't know where to begin. It's like that when I give a speech."

The problem is that so many people develop a speech or talk using the same methods they employed to write term papers in school or college. That is, they try to fill up as many pages as possible. In many cases they got good grades on such papers—the professor was giving them a mark for effort. The professor, of course, was able to skim over the repetitions and irrelevancies. But a listening audience can't skim. A listening audience is a captive audience. But the members of that audience do have a line of defense—they can tune out. And that is precisely what they will do if you have not edited yourself properly beforehand.

That is one reason why I advocate the use of 5 × 8 cards when preparing a speech. The limited space available on such cards acts as a psychological inhibitor on any tendency to spew out reams of information. That limited space is a constant reminder that self-editing is necessary. Some students tell me the only way they can organize their ideas is to write page after page and then cut out the irrelevant material. But this is a self-defeating way of writing a speech. One does not write a novel and cut it back to a short story. *They are different forms, with different demands.* A term paper and a speech likewise have very different purposes and demands.

When you are preparing a speech you must stick to your word budget, constantly checking the number of words you have written down against the time allotted for each section. In filling out the personal, corporate, or historical models, keep in mind that it takes approximately one minute to speak 150 words. Assume that your background section will take up one minute of your completed speech. Both models contain seven questions, but you are asked to give three examples to the sixth question, What happened as a result? Thus your background material comprises ten units. With one minute of speaking time, each unit should consist of about fifteen words, with three units allowed under the sixth question. In doing the following exercise, therefore, keep those word and time limits firmly in mind.

As we previously mentioned, it is best to know the introductory section of your speech well enough so that you do not have to look at your cards until you come to the background section.

What if you feel that you *must* read your entire talk? A New York speech coach advises, "Don't read your speech, or you will sound stilted." But this all-or-nothing attitude is unrealistic and serves only further to discourage inexperienced speakers from ever taking the risk of speaking in public.

Common sense will tell you it is certainly better to feel secure, even if you do sound a bit stilted. And you do not have to sound stilted reading from a card. I have seen many professional speakers read their speeches without a trace of stiltedness. Of course, during your rehearsal at home always make the effort to speak your introduction and your topic and thesis sentences without reading. But if you feel that not using your cards will cause too much anxiety, then by all means begin by reading. With each new talk, as you become more familiar with the presenting experience, you can try to look away from your cards more and more. Remember that you are learning; you don't have to be perfect the very first time—or even the tenth time. However, if you use the Talk-Power model, including the word budget principle, even if you do read from a card, *your talks will sound professional* from the very first time you stand in front of a group and speak.

Exercise Fourteen: Presenting a Background

1. Fill out either the personal, corporate, or historical model on the previous pages.
2. Using that information, write out a brief story (150 words maximum) on a 5 × 8 card.
3. Take out the cards on which you have previously written your joke or anecdote, your topic sentence, and your thesis sentence. Add your new background card. Write REST PERIOD—COUNT TO FIVE after the last word of your background.
4. Again, go through a complete rehearsal step by step including all the techniques you have learned to help you concentrate, to slow down your responses, and to put you in touch with your body.

Rehearsal

- *Very slowly* pull yourself up to your feet.
- Stand in place and balance your weight evenly on both feet.
- Step first with your right foot, then your left, and stop on both feet. Concentrate on your fingertips. Do this until you've walked up to the front of your imaginary audience.
- *Slowly* turn and face your imaginary audience, keeping your arms at your sides.

- Do your checklist:
  - My head feels . . .
  - My eyes are . . .
  - My mouth is . . .
  - My shoulders are . . .
  - My neck is . . .
  - My chest feels . . .
  - My heart is . . .
  - My arms are . . .
  - My stomach is . . .
  - My hands feel . . .
  - My legs feel . . .
  - My knees are . . .
  - The bottom of my feet are . . .
- Tell your joke. Pause.
- Give your topic sentence and pause, then your thesis sentence and pause.
- Turn and read your background cards, remembering to look at the audience from time to time.
- Now walk back to your seat. Sit quietly for ten gentle breaths.

Repeat this sequence until ten minutes have gone by. (Use a kitchen timer.)

Progress Report

Date	Time	Strong Spot	Weak Spot	Comment	Calm–Nervous (1–10)

CHAPTER 8

How to Think Systematically (The Point Section)

Barbara G. spends a great deal of time and energy avoiding any kind of public speaking. This is difficult to do because Barbara works for the educational department of a government agency, where presentations and seminars are frequent.

Many years ago in college, Barbara was told by her teachers and friends that when she got up to speak her talks seemed endless. Her points were not clear, and her disorganization was so apparent that she simply had to do something about it.

So Barbara took public speaking courses, in which she was taught how to develop the main points in the body of her speech. But this information has not been too helpful. Although Barbara is quite intelligent, she continues to feel that her talks are too long, off the track, and boring, and she still has no idea how to organize her points.

As a result Barbara stays in the same job slot year after year, deliberately avoiding promotion because the next position in her line includes weekly off-site presentations in which she would be expected to give summary talks to research groups connected with her agency. Barbara has "solved" her problem by making sure she will never have to expose herself by talking in public.

Barbara's public speaking teachers have given her a great deal of support, positive feedback, and general advice. But they have concerned themselves with the theory of speechmaking, rather than with procedural techniques. Barbara has never learned a systematic and detailed step-by-step method for *organizing and developing* ideas for a talk. When Barbara begins to compose her talks, she is so overwhelmed by masses of facts, statistics, and references that she loses control over her material. She never establishes a strong point of view or moves in a clear direction.

By using the Talk-Power system, however, even someone like Barbara can learn to write a speech that presents facts and statistics in a controlled way, so that each *makes its point* instead of being just one more item on an endless list of information. The secret lies in tying each fact, each point, to the topic and thesis sentences with which you begin your talk.

The Talk-Power Formula

Beginning:	*Introductory Paragraph* (1)
	Topic Sentence (2)
	Thesis Sentence (3)
Middle:	*Background* (4)
	Point Section (5) Point A Point B Point C Point D
	Climax (6)
End:	*Conclusion* (7)

APPROACHING THE POINT SECTION (5)

The purpose of the point section is to teach you **how to build on your topic and thesis sentences so that you do not drift away from your central theme.** This approach can guide you into developing an interesting as well as informative speech in a systematic manner.

The point section of your talk divides your topic sentence into several such points or subheadings.

Let's look at an example.

During a recent dispute about the price of a subway token, one of my students had to prepare a talk for his weekly current events club. Here is how he organized his topic—*the subway situation*—into points or subheadings:

Topic: Today I am going to talk about the subway situation.

Thesis: I think the token should not be increased in price.

Background: . . . .

Point Section: Point 1. History of the subways in New York City
Point 2. The poor conditions of the subways
Point 3. The importance of the subways in New York

He was to speak for ten minutes. With one minute for his entrance and one minute for his background, he had about eight minutes left for the rest of his talk, or about two and one-half minutes for each of his points. That works out to 375 words for each point.

Using this time-controlled structure, he was able to outline his ideas and fill them in with the proper research to develop an interesting and informative talk that fell within his time limitation.

The question arises, how did my student arrive at these particular points? After all, there are literally dozens of different subheadings he might have chosen. The answer lies in a technique used for adding variety and interest to a talk. This technique is called brainstorming.

Brainstorming

Brainstorming is a process for coming up with as many creative ideas as freely and as quickly as possible in a given time frame—*without passing judgment* on any of the ideas.

Write down your topic sentence on the first line of a card, then setting a kitchen timer to ten minutes. Now brainstorm. The idea is to write as many subheadings as possible for your topic down on your card. All this is to be done within the ten-minute time limit. Include all ideas, no matter how ridiculous or silly. (It is good to be as imaginative and playful as possible, since you are the only one who will see this copy of your list.)

At the end of ten minutes, the brainstorming session is over. The next step is to go over the list, eliminating inappropriate subheadings. Keep paring down the list until you have the number of points you need for your talk. Usually three or four subheadings will fill the bill.

Here is the list that my student developed about subways before he came up with his final list of four:

- Subways of the future
- Subways are for sleeping
- Violence on the subway
- The runaway subway
- Subways and the elderly
- Subways and the very young

- Noise and the subway
- Sex and the subways
- Crime and the subways
- Movies and the subways
- Laughter on the subways
- The federal government and the subways
- The subway cost
- The subway token
- Meeting men on the subways
- Meeting women on the subways
- Abolishing the subways
- History of the subways
- A new subway
- The grafitti on the subways
- Subway police
- Subway secrets
- Subways in other cities
- Subways in other countries
- Before subways
- My memories of the subways years ago
- Poor conditions of the subways
- Politicians and the subways
- Corruption and the subways
- Jobs and the subways
- The Transit Union
- Importance of the subway
- Teenage crime and the subways
- Subway accidents

By a process of elimination he was able to select his final points:

- The history of the subway
- The federal government and the subways
- The importance of the subway to New York City

The order of the points chosen should always move from the least dramatic or exciting to the most interesting or important. Remember it is *your* speech. You must decide what that order should be.

Chunking

In selecting your points, do not exceed seven points, including your climax, no matter how long your speech is. This is not an arbitrary number. It is based on the amount of information that the human brain can absorb at a given time.

As Peter Russell writes in *The Brain Book,* "Immediate memory is limited to about seven "chunks" of information. Most people can remember about seven numbers in a row, seven colors, seven shapes or seven of any other item. So if you need to remember more than seven items, it's better to organize them into a smaller number of chunks."

If you attempt to make more than seven points in a speech, not only will you have trouble remembering them but your audience will find it difficult to absorb them.

Exercise Fifteen: Choosing Your Points for a Seven-Minute Speech

1. Look at your topic sentence card. Set a kitchen timer to ten minutes. Now quickly write as many different subheadings as you can think of that *relate to your topic sentence.* Do not eliminate any points because they seem silly or inappropriate. You want your unconscious creative mind to be as open and uncensored as possible.

When the timer goes off stop writing.

2. Eliminate the subheadings you cannot use until you have four subheadings left.

3. Now arrange the list of four points in order of importance—the least important first, the most important last. Note each point on a separate card. (Be sure to number your cards.)

DEVELOPING YOUR POINTS

Once you've chosen your points, write out on separate cards all of the information (several data, statistics, anecdotal references, dates, etc.) that falls under the heading of each point. Work on one card at a time, as if it were an independent unit. Put your information into an easily followed logical order.

When you have developed your first subheading in 150 words, put that card aside and go on to the next card, which has the next subheading on it. Work on this in the same way until you have developed all four subheadings you have decided to use.

This is what one fully developed point or subheading might look like. (The topic sentence and thesis is included to give you some orientation to the point.)

Topic: Tonight I am going to talk about personal organization.
Thesis: I believe that a personal system for organization can enhance your life.
Point 1: The importance of a calendar

The system's main component is this year's calendar. This calendar is used for *goal clarification.* It forces us to look at ourselves and our goals and to make plans to meet them. The calendar gives us a timetable in which to complete these goals. This is important because it takes the emphasis off specific daily tasks like "take the car to the repair shop" and puts it on more important activities.

It is very easy to get caught in the trap of completing every chore on our daily lists and yet, at the end of the year, feeling like we haven't accomplished anything. At this point this speaker showed the audience an example of a calendar with various schedules and an explanation:

Monthly schedule
Daily schedule
Phone list

You now have the basics for an organizational system that will clarify your life goals and thus result in a more enjoyable life. How you incorporate the system into your own life depends on your individual style and needs. Some of you may like the flexibility that a three-ring binder gives you. Others, preferring less bulk, may opt for a small pocket system.

By now you should have amassed a number of facts and figures under the various subheadings. However, facts and figures have no meaning unless they are tied together by a *central idea.*

Beverly G. is a social worker at a municipal hospital. Beverly and a colleague were planning to give a series of workshops on stress reduction, a subject area in which Beverly, as a therapist, has a great deal of expertise.

After the first workshop, Beverly contacted me in great distress. Her portion of the workshop had been a total failure. She felt embarrassed, and the thought of having to do it again made her ill.

Beverly tried to explain her problem. She had amassed a great deal of information—notes, facts, etc.—all of which made sense to her when she was doing her rehearsal. But she found herself unable to get them across to her actual audience.

What had gone wrong? How could we begin to sort out Beverly's difficulty with her presentation?

When I began analyzing Beverly's speech in terms of the our Talk-Power model, I discovered that although she had reams of information, she had never formulated a central point of view or thesis. As a result, there was no way of introducing a theme or making connections between the facts she had to present.

I pointed this out to her. She developed a thesis statement for her next presentation and found she was able to break up her talk into a series of subheadings. By repeating her thesis as a theme in each subheading (point), the once totally disorganized mass of information was infused with meaning. A very interesting presentation developed. It was warmly received, and her desire to do more presentations and workshops was greatly increased.

The Thesis Message

Each time you introduce a new point or subheading to the audience, you should restate the original thesis sentence somewhere within that point. This restated sentence is called the *thesis message.* It reiterates the theme of your talk, the central message that you would like your audience to retain. It is the connecting link that brings meaning to all the facts and statistics that you are presenting in your point section.

Finding the connection between your points and your thesis is the final step in writing the point section of your speech. It should be undertaken *after* all your points have been fully developed.

Let us take a point and examine it fully, so that you can grasp the principles involved. If you know how to develop one point in detail, you will be able to develop the rest along the same lines.

Exercise Sixteen: How to Connect a Point to Your Thesis

1. Take a card with a fully developed point written on it—150 words—and read it over carefully. Now go back to your thesis sentence and read that again. Look for a connection between your point and the thesis sentence.
2. In one or at most two sentences, express the connecting idea in writing. *Use key words from the original thesis.* You have just formulated your thesis message.
3. Now find a place in your point where you can appropriately slip this sentence in so that it makes sense and blends in with the rest of the information.

To give you a better idea of how this is done, let us go back to the example just used for developing a point and let us now insert a thesis message.

> *Topic:* Tonight I am going to talk about a system for personal organization.
> *Thesis:* I believe that a personal system for organization can enhance your life.
> *Point 1:* The importance of a calendar
>
> The system's main component is this year's calendar. This calendar is used for goal clarification. It forces us to look at ourselves and our goals and to make plans to meet them. The calendar gives us a timetable in which to complete these goals. This is important because it takes the emphasis off specific daily tasks like "take the car to the repair shop" and puts it on more important activities.
>
> It is very easy to get caught in the trap of completing every

chore on our daily lists and yet, at the end of the year, feeling like we haven't accomplished anything.

Monthly schedule
Daily schedule
Phone list

Message: You now have the basics for an organizational system that will clarify your life goals and enhance your life.

How you incorporate the system into your own life depends on your individual style and needs. Some of you may like the flexibility that a three-ring binder gives you. Others, preferring less bulk, may opt for a small pocket system.

The most important thing to remember about developing a point is that no matter what your subheading is about, it must always tie into your thesis in some way. In other words, if your subheading is about the importance of a calendar, and your thesis sentence states that a personal system for organization can enhance your life, there must be one sentence in your subheading in which you repeat the essence of your thesis sentence using key words from your thesis. When you repeat the gist of your thesis sentence in a subheading, it becomes a thesis message.

Here is an example of how Dr. Lisa W., one of my students, developed a point for a talk about traveling by train.

Let us begin at the beginning, with her introduction.

Introduction: A staggering number of Americans suffer from motion sickness each year. Thousands get seasick on boats, tens of thousands get airsick on planes. Hundreds of thousands get carsick, and millions of our fellow Americans get bus sick each year.

(Pause)

Topic: Tonight I'd like to talk to you about trains.

(Pause)

Thesis: I'm convinced that trains offer the traveler far more advantages than any other form of transportation.

(Pause)

Background: I first became interested in trains as a child when, to my amazement, I discovered that it was actually possible to travel and not get nauseous. This was after years of throwing up in cars, buses, boats, and planes. Not only did I feel wonderful in trains, but I could even eat and read with impunity. At every opportunity thereafter I traveled by train.

My most pleasant experience was using a Eurailpass in Scandinavia several years ago. In Denmark I traveled in a gorgeous train with mahogany paneling and furniture, plush upholstered chairs, and brass light fixtures.

In Norway the trains were sleek and modern, with lovely dining and sleeping cars, and of course, the scenery we passed was breathtaking. I look forward to seeing more of this country and Europe—by train, of course.

(Pause)

Point: Train travel is exceptionally comfortable. You can read or write in your seat, or just enjoy the scenery. When you tire of sitting, you can walk from car to car and stand a while, perhaps opening a window to let in some fresh air.

If you are hungry, you can relax in the dining car and have a delicious meal amid beautiful surroundings. And at night, you can sleep comfortably in a cozy private car and wake up refreshed in the morning.

Thesis Message: One advantage of traveling by train is that it is far more comfortable than traveling by any other means of transportation.

If you will look back to the beginning of this talk, you will see that the original thesis message was: *"I'm convinced that trains offer the traveler far more advantages than any other form of transportation."* Can you see how the thesis message echos the original statement?

If you choose to repeat your thesis message in the last line, that is fine. However, the thesis message can also appear in the first line of a point or in the middle. It can be a question or a statement. The form or placement of the thesis message does not matter as long as it appears in some form *once in each of your points.*

It is precisely because the thesis message is to be repeated that it is vital to limit the thesis to one and only one, message or point of view.

One of my students was preparing a travel presentation for her agency. Her thesis was *"England for the sightseer cannot be rivaled and so everyone should go there."* When it came to developing this thesis she ran into problems. Why? She was riding two different horses at the same time. It was only when she chose to develop the single idea that England could not be rivaled as a sightseers' haven that her task became clarified. The idea that everyone should go there had to be eliminated because it was in fact a second thesis.

Exercise Seventeen: Completing Your Points

Go back to your subheading cards. Working on one subheading at a time, do just as you did in Exercise Sixteen, where you learned how to connect your thesis message to a subheading.

1. Read the material in your subheading.
2. Go back to your thesis sentence and read it.
3. Find the appropriate place in each one of your subheadings where you can place your thesis message so that it makes sense.

If you cannot find a place in what you have written where your thesis sentence makes sense, then there is something wrong with your point. Usually it means that you have strayed so far away from the topic that you are no longer writing the talk that you set out to give. In this case, scrap the point, go back to your topic sentence, and find another point that is within the limits of your chosen topic.

4. Once you are satisfied that your point makes sense and has restated the thesis message in a sensible place, work through the other cards in exactly the same way.

When you have finished developing each of your points individually, you will find that you do not need transitional phrases or bridges as you go from one point to the next. The sense of continuity is created by repetition of the thesis sentence that you have included in each point.

When you rehearse your speech, you will need a five-second pause between each point. Remember to write this pause in at the end of each point. Write in big letters on your card REST PERIOD—COUNT TO FIVE.

PUTTING YOUR POINTS IN ORDER

When you have finished developing each of your points in turn, gather all of your cards together and read them through to make certain they are arranged in a dynamic order, from least exciting to most exciting. Number each card in accordance with the order you decide on.

The importance of building your speech to its most exciting moment can be made clearer with a simple analogy. If you have ever watched a baseball game in which one team is ahead by seven runs in the eighth inning, you will have observed that the spectators start leaving early. The moment of climax in the game, the big inning, has already occurred. With a speech, if you offer the most exciting part of your speech too soon, the audience will stay in their seats—they don't want to be so rude as to walk out. But they will begin to tune out what you are saying.

Exercise Eighteen: Rehearsal

1. Sit in your chair. Center yourself.
2. Put your card in your lap and rest your hands on your lap. Try to feel the pulse in your fingertips without shaking your hands. Concentrate on the tingling in your fingertips.
3. Take your card in your hand, and *very slowly* pull yourself up to your feet.
4. Stand in place and balance your weight evenly on both feet.
5. Begin to walk naturally, slowly until you reach the front.
6. *Slowly* turn and face your imaginary audience, keeping your arms at your sides.
7. Do your checklist: My head feels . . .
   My eyes are . . .
   My mouth is . . .
   My shoulders are . . .
   My neck is . . .
   My chest feels . . .
   My heart is . . .
   My arms are . . .
   My stomach is . . .
   My hands feel . . .
   My legs feel . . .
   My knees are . . .
   The bottom of my feet are . . .
8. Now tell your joke. Pause.

9. Give your topic sentence and pause, then your thesis sentence and pause.

10. Read from your cards, looking up at the audience from time to time, until you have gone through your background and point sections.

11. Now walk back to your seat. Sit quietly for ten gentle breaths.

Begin again, repeating this entire sequence one more time.

Progress Report

Date	Time	Strong Spot	Weak Spot	Comment	Calm–Nervous (1–10)

The Talk-Power Formula

Beginning:	*Introductory Paragraph* (1)
	Topic Sentence (2)
	Thesis Sentence (3)
Middle:	*Background* (4)
	Point Section (5) Point A Point B Point C Point D
	Climax (6)
End:	*Conclusion* (7)

THE CLIMAX (6)—YOUR LAST POINT

The very last point you make is your climax. **The climax is your final opportunity to get through to your audience**—to try to convince, persuade, or arouse them. It is your last opportunity to achieve your intention.

Even if the full force of your thesis has not been projected yet, the climax gives you a chance to drive it home, to excite your listeners.

Many people save the high point of their talk for the conclusion. But this is not recommended in the Talk-Power model. A conclusion is simply a summing up and leave-taking. Once you have come to the conclusion, your foot is halfway out the door, as it were, and it is both useless and bad form for you to start a new pitch at that juncture.

The place to give it your all is the climax.

You can create a climactic effect in a number of ways —an anecdote of dramatic intensity, quotes from a newspaper article, a shocking statistic, news about the losing or the saving of money, the story of a miraculous cure or an awful disappointment, a startling announcement, etc. These are all possible climax techniques.

The climax should be the peak of interest and excitement in your talk.

As we mentioned earlier, the order of points is always from the least important to what you consider the most important. This is in order to insure the interest and attention of the audience. You keep building and intensifying their involvement by making your presentation progressively more exciting.

In terms of your word budget, remember that *the climax is a part of your point section,* not a separate section in itself. The fact that the climax is intended to be the most dramatic and exciting moment of your talk does *not* mean you should expend extra words on it. If you allow yourself to become wordy at this juncture, you are likely to lose the impact of your climax.

As with all the other points in the point section, the climax should contain your thesis message. It may be in the form of a statement or a question, and it may come at the beginning, in the middle, or at the end. But it must be included.

Here is an example of a climax, written by Diane K. for a Talk-Power seminar. Diane was giving a demonstration talk about growing avocados.

> If you follow these instructions, you will have a gorgeous, lush tree within two years that will grow quickly and beautifully. You will feel very proud of yourself for having been patient and courageous in the early months of growing an avocado.
>
> Just imagine yourself walking on your terrace with friends who are filled with awe at the many lovely plants in your garden. They point to the avocado trees and gasp, "What's that beautiful plant?"
>
> You smile demurely, accepting the praise gracefully, and remark, "Why, this is my prize avocado tree. I grew it myself."

Exercise Nineteen: Strengthening the Climax

Go back to your speech and look at your four points. Now take your last point and dress it up, dramatizing it so that it becomes even more exciting than it was. This can be done by using more dramatic language, more visually colorful descriptions, more active verbs, etc. If you feel that your last point is just not salvageable as an exciting climax, then substitute a new point, either an anecdote or a piece of information that can truly serve as the high point of your talk.

Be sure that your thesis message is included in your climax and that you put REST PERIOD—COUNT TO FIVE at the end of the point.

Now you are ready for a full rehearsal.

Exercise Twenty: Rehearsal

1. Sit in your chair. Center yourself.
2. With your card in your lap, concentrate on the tingling in your fingertips.
3. Take your card in your hand and *very slowly* pull yourself up to your feet.
4. Stand in place, and balance your weight evenly on both feet.
5. Walk naturally, slowly up to the front of your imaginary audience.
6. *Slowly* turn and face your imaginary audience, keeping your arms at your sides.
7. Run through your checklist: My head feels . . .
   My eyes are . . .
   My mouth is . . .
   My shoulders are . . .
   etc.
8. Give your introduction. Pause.
9. Using your cards, complete the remainder of your talk up through the climax. Remember to pause each time you come to a new section or point. Be sure to look up at the audience from time to time.

Progress Report

Date	Time	Strong Spot	Weak Spot	Comment	Calm–Nervous (1–10)

CHAPTER 9

How to Say Goodbye (The Conclusion)

Saying goodbye is often a problem. Perhaps you have experienced the jolt of listening to a speaker who suddenly, out of nowhere, uttered an abrupt "Thank you" and left the stage with the speed of a frightened rabbit. A more common experience is to be forced to listen to "final remarks" that go on endlessly, as the speaker sorts through the odds and ends of leftover notes clutched in his hands, talking himself to death and his audience into insensibility.

The lack of understanding about how to say goodbye when speaking in public is in some ways curious. After all, most people know perfectly well how to conclude a business letter or telephone call. The explanation for the difficulties these same people encounter when making a speech once again lies in the strangeness of the public speaking experience. Thus, as with the other sections of a speech, knowing exactly what needs to be accomplished in making a conclusion, and having clear, definite rules to follow in carrying out that intention, can spell the difference between a graceful exit and a meandering or overly abrupt one.

The purpose of your conclusion is to inform the

audience that your talk is over, to give a brief summation of your past points, to repeat your thesis message, and then to leave.

The conclusion is the last section of your speech. It is separated from the final word of your climax by a brief pause of a few seconds. Just as your entrance remark at the start of your talk serves to introduce you to your audience and to give audience members time to adjust to your presence, so the conclusion serves to prepare the audience for your departure. Now you let them know you are giving up your position at the center of attention.

I believe that no matter how long your speech has lasted, the conclusion should never run more than 150 words. If you cannot sum up in 150 words or less, it probably means that the body of your speech consisted of too many ill-focused points to begin with. However, don't be too abbreviated in your close, or it will come too abruptly for your audience. A good rule of thumb is to construct your conclusion to run between 75 and 150 words—neither too short nor too long.

The Talk-Power Formula

Beginning:	*Introductory Paragraph* (1)
	Topic Sentence (2)
	Thesis Sentence (3)
Middle:	*Background* (4)
	Point Section (5) Point A Point B Point C Point D
	Climax (6)
End:	*Conclusion* (7)

A conclusion *never* gives any new information. Facts or statements that have not been fully clarified in the body of your speech should be avoided. You may say, "But I want to give the audience something to think about." Well, if you haven't already given them something to think about in the body of your speech, you have missed your opportunity; your moment to do so has passed. Your conclusion only lists or sums up your main points. Do not introduce anything new for discussion or consideration.

Keep your conclusion calm and smooth. Avoid bombastic or shocking endings. They confuse and agitate an audience, as well as yourself.

TYPES OF CONCLUSIONS

There are three possible variations or forms that a conclusion can properly take:

1. You can summarize the main points of your talk. In that case, no more than one sentence should be devoted to any given point.
2. You can conclude with an anecdote or a story (150 words maximum) that drives your point home.
3. You can conclude with an apt quotation, tying it into your thesis.

Examples of Conclusions

Summary

In conclusion I would like to summarize the main points of my talk:

1. I want to stress the fact that the most critical element in the fight against this disease is education of both the health professional and the public.

2. Although statistics show that one out of fourteen women develop breast cancer and this high number is frightening, it is important to educate families without arousing anxiety.

3. In order to achieve better treatment and rehabilitation, early detection and diagnosis is of the utmost importance.

4. If all women would take just a few minutes of their time at least once a month to examine their breasts, thousands of breast cancer deaths could be avoided.

(Repeat thesis.)

Story

In conclusion let me share with you this anecdote:

Bob Gannon was a tough kid from a tough neighborhood. He joined the United States Navy at seventeen, where he became involved in an amateur boxing program. Bob got married at twenty and stayed active in the Golden Gloves and other amateur boxing events. He had grown to five feet nine inches and one hundred fifty-nine pounds. On one particular night in October 1978, Bob Gannon faced his antagonist and stepped forward. He threw two punches, the second of which landed on his rival's head. His opponent dropped, never to rise again. Bob's opponent, his eight-year-old son, was dead—another victim of child abuse.

Quotation

I am now at the end of my talk, and I would like to leave you with the words of a song that have made a great impression on me. It is from a John Lennon song and it says, "Life is something that happens while you were busy making other plans."

I think that we must begin dealing with what is really happening in the economy, rather than listening to plans, and statistics.

The *summary* conclusion here ends with a restatement of the thesis.

In the sample *story* conclusion, you will note that the anecdote used illustrates forcefully an instance of child abuse. In fact, the speech here revolved about a need to show greater awareness of the problem of child abuse. The conclusion thus refers back to the thesis.

In the sample *quotation* conclusion, the final sentence is actually a repeat of the speaker's thesis.

Every conclusion should somehow reinforce or repeat the thesis that you want your audience to respond to.

Exercise Twenty-one

Select one form of conclusion and write a brief conclusion for the speech that you have been working on throughout your training program. Remember to include mention of your thesis.

____

____

____

____

____

____

____

DID YOU ACCOMPLISH WHAT YOU SET OUT TO DO?

Reviewing Your Intention

If you will recall, in Chapter 5 we discussed your intention in writing your talk. We asked you to identify that intention by stating what it was you wanted your audience *to do* once they had heard your speech. Now that you have concluded your speech, it is important to go back and check your speech by asking this question: Is my thesis really going to motivate the audience to take action or react in the way that I would like them to?

Bernice A., in a drive to recruit blood donors, used as her thesis: "I think that plasma is the liquid of life." However, when she had completed her speech, she realized that while everyone would agree that plasma is the liquid of life, in order to motivate her audience to sign up for her drive, she needed a stronger, more direct thesis. She therefore changed her thesis to "I believe we must all pitch in to make this drive a success." It was really not necessary for her to change anything in her speech aside from substituting her new thesis and new thesis messages in each point of the original.

In a speech that Sally T. had prepared for her local block association, she used the thesis "I believe that traffic lights are important for pedestrians as well as drivers." Well, of course, traffic lights are important. Who would disagree with such a statement? The point that Sally really wanted to make was that broken traffic lights should immediately be reported and repaired. When she changed her thesis to "I believe that a broken traffic light is a hazard to the community," her speech became stronger. She was more effective in motivating her audience to form a permanent watchdog committee for the reporting of broken traffic lights.

The following exercise will guide you in determining that you are actually doing what you set out to do, that is, fulfilling your intention.

Exercise Twenty-two: Visualizing Your Intention

1. Go back to the speech you've been working on, and answer this question: *Ideally, what is it that you would like your audience to do after they hear your talk?*

I would like my audience to ______________________

____

2. Please write in the *thesis sentence* that you used in your speech: ______________________________________

____

Is your thesis stated in such a way that it will really help you to accomplish your intention? (Yes) (No)

Is your thesis as clear . . . important . . . fully energetic . . . forceful . . . specific as it can be? (Yes) (No)

3. If both answers above are *yes,* leave the thesis sentence alone.

If either answer is *no,* what can you do to improve your thesis sentence?

New thesis sentence: ______________________________

____

____

TALK-POWER FORMULA OVERVIEW

The following overview chart will give you a *total* picture of how a speech is put together according to the Talk-Power Formula.

On the left-hand side of the page you will find a brief description of each section of the speech. On the right-hand side, the *self-talk* column will give you a thought-by-thought analysis that fully explains the intentions of the speaker as he goes through the various sections.

Now you are ready to write a complete new speech.

Exercise Twenty-three: Preparing a Complete Speech

Let's imagine that you have just been assigned a talk, either by your boss, your organization, or your club.

Using the Action Formula, organize a complete speech about a topic you are very familiar with.

1. Pick your topic.

Here is a selection of topic possibilities:

- Your favorite restaurant
- A how-to
- Your system for personal money management
- Your point of view about the economy
- Selling a product
- A controversial subject
- A work-related issue
- A training talk
- A recruitment talk
- The importance of religion in your life
- Your favorite sports team
- Your job

The Talk-Power Formula and How It Works

Part 1—The Introduction

Description of Section		Self-Talk
1. **Introductory Remark** The introductory remark begins your talk. It can be a joke, a shocking statement, rhetorical question, quotation, etc. It should have no more than 150 words (one minute of speaking).	A joke (Pause)	"This joke will help the audience to focus attention on me and what I am saying with very little feeling of pressure on them."
2. **Topic Sentence** The topic sentence introduces the general direction of the speech. It follows the last line of the introductory remark and is one sentence.	"Today I am going to talk about. . . ." (Pause)	"Now that the audience has had a chance to hear and see me, I am going to direct their attention to the *general area* of my talk."

Description of Section		Self-Talk
3. **Thesis Sentence** The thesis sentence introduces your central point of view about the topic. It follows the topic sentence and is also a single declarative sentence. It begins with "I think" or "I feel" or "I believe."	"I think that. . . ." (Pause)	"Now I need to share my real feelings about the topic so the audience will be able to follow my reasoning with clarity and comfort. If they know exactly what my point of view is, they will be able to understand and remember what I am saying more easily."
Part 2—The Body		
4. **Background** The background section answers one of three questions: 1. Why am I talking about the topic? *(personal approach)* 2. Why is my company interested in the topic? *(corporate approach)*		"Now I need to share something about myself, because I want the audience to feel that I am a person just as they are, that I am not a stranger. The more they find me or my topic interesting, the more willing they will be to listen to what I have to say later on in my talk. I do not

3. Why is the topic in itself interesting? (*historical approach*—a brief overview of the history of the topic) The background has a maximum of 150 words and a minimum of 75 words.	(Pause)	need to defend my point of view in this section."
5. **The Point Section** You may have from one to seven points in your talk, depending on the amount of time you wish to speak.	*First point*	"Now I am beginning to develop my talk through a step-by-step or point-by-point procedure. I think the audience is really ready to give me their full attention, and I can begin to introduce more complex ideas. Of course, repeating my thesis at some point will help me maintain my direction, so that I do not stray too far away from my central point of view."
Point A This is the first point you have selected from your brainstorming about the topic. You will develop this point in 150 words or more, depending on how long you wish to speak.	(Pause)	

Description of Section		Self-Talk
Point B This is the second point. It is a little more exciting than the first point. Once again, remember to include your thesis sentence wherever it works. (If you wish to make this point longer, eliminate the third point.)	*Second point* (Pause)	"Now I will spell out another aspect of my topic for my audience. When I repeat my thesis sentence, it sounds like a theme that becomes more and more familiar to my listeners."
Point C This is the third point. It will further develop the talk. The use of visuals here will surely heighten the interest of the audience. (But watch your word budget.)	*Third point* (Pause)	"I have tried to present all relevant aspects of this topic so that my audience can get as full a picture as possible. I feel as if by now the pieces all fit together and my audience can see the reasoning behind my thesis."

6. **Climax**
This is the high point of the talk. Although this climax has all of the characteristics of a point, remember that this is your last point—it must be as dramatic and exciting as possible. Be sure to repeat your thesis sentence in some manner.

"This climax will really help to motivate my audience. I have slowly been building up to this high point in my talk. I can really feel them listening intently to every word I am saying. This is my last chance to drive home my point. I want my audience to remember what I came here to tell them—and to remember me."

(Pause)

Part 3—Conclusion

7. **Conclusion**
This is the very last section of the talk. You are preparing to leave by summing up the main points of your talk or by using one of the other devices for saying goodbye to your audience with dignity *and brevity.* (Use no more than 150 words in the conclusion.)

"My conclusion is telling the audience that my speech is practically over. It has been an exciting trip. Now I am slowly beginning to unwind and descend. I feel a sense of unity with the audience—I have done my very best to share my message in an interesting and informative manner."

2. Prepare your introductory paragraph (150 words maximum-75 words minimum).

3. Write out your topic sentence—"Today I am going to talk about. . ."

4. Write out your thesis sentence—"I think that. . ."

5. Compose your background paragraph (150 words maximum/75 words minimum)—why you are giving this talk, how you became involved with this subject, why your company is interested in this subject, etc.

6. Brainstorm twenty subheadings. Give yourself ten minutes only to do this.

7. Pick out four interesting subheadings that you want to develop in your speech. (Save one subheading for your climax.)

8. Develop each subheading (150 words maximum/75 words minimum). Be sure to include or mention your thesis in one sentence in each subheading.

9. Add your climax. Remember this should be the most exciting, emotionally arousing section in your speech.

10. Finish with your conclusion (150 words maximum/ 75 words minimum).

11. Insert the words REST PERIOD—COUNT TO FIVE at the end of each section.

12. Now go through a complete rehearsal.

Rehearsal

- Sit in your chair. Center yourself.
- With your card in your lap, concentrate on the tingling in your fingertips.
- Take your card in your hand and *very slowly* pull yourself up to your feet.
- Stand in place and balance your weight evenly on both feet.

- Walk slowly and naturally up to the front of your imaginary audience, concentrating on your fingertips as you move.
- *Slowly* turn and face your imaginary audience, keeping your arms at your sides.
- Run through your checklist:
  My head feels . . .
  My eyes are . . .
  My mouth is . . .
  etc.
- Now begin your presentation. Try not to look at your cards until you come to your background. When you come to your background section, you may read from your cards, but do not forget to look at your audience from time to time.
- Go through your entire speech, remembering to take a pause after each section, then return to your chair.

Progress Report

Date	Time	Strong Spot	Weak Spot	Comment	Calm–Nervous (1–10)

CHAPTER 10

How to Use Visual Aids

If you are planning a talk that will run five minutes or more, you would be well advised to consider using some kind of a visual aid as part of your presentation.

Visual aids (or visuals) are any pictures, objects, artifacts, flip-charts, illustrations, transparencies, or projections that you might show to your audience during the course of your talk.

Some people seem to think audiovisual bombardment can cover up poor presentational style. It can't. Imagine the President's annual State of the Union Address written, produced, and presented by Walt Disney Studios. Then imagine what your reaction would be to a stammering leader who could do no more than point at the Disney production material. You will immediately understand why hopes of hiding behind visual aids can lead to audiovisual overkill. Your anxiety may be relieved, but you will not effectively sell your product or ideas.

With this in mind, let us now consider the matter of visuals from a realistic and sensible perspective.

The purpose of visuals is to add variety to your talk and to illustrate and further clarify your point of view. However, if your visuals are handled sloppily or nervously, or if your visuals are too small to be seen comfortably by the audience, they can become more of a hindrance than a help.

What is it that makes a visual usable? First of all, any pictures and posters must be large enough for your audience to see them. An effective technique when using posters is to tape the poster to a blackboard, then cover the poster with a large piece of paper that can easily be pulled off when you want to display it to the audience.

One of my students, in a talk on escalating OPEC oil prices, used a large chart with OPEC prices arranged in successive vertical strips about an inch wide. Each strip represented one year's prices. He then taped an inch-wide strip of paper over each column. As he moved from year to year in his speech, he dramatically pulled off each strip of paper to reveal the escalating costs of oil. His technique was very effective and worked to illustrate his thesis in a new and creative manner.

In considering the handling of visuals, the presentational mode must be emphasized once again. You are not operating in a social mode. Therefore, the way that you pick up objects, how you hold them in front of an audience, and the speed at which you move a pointer across a chart or a map must be different than would be the case in a casual social situation.

All visuals are used for demonstration. To demonstrate something, you must be very conscious of the weight of the object you are holding. And the speed at which you move or manipulate the object must be slow enough so that you can be sure the audience's attention is directed exactly where you want it.

A magician using sleight of hand moves so quickly that the audience does not have time to see what he is doing. You want the opposite effect. When showing a visual to accompany a speech, you must move with exaggerated slowness, so that the audience can see exactly what it is that you wish to show them. This is especially important when using graphs and maps. The presenter who quickly moves his or her pointer or pencil across a map or graph can be sure nobody in the audience is following him.

All moves made with a pointer should be in slow motion. Because your rate of talking will be normal and not as slow as your movement, there must be pauses in your talk so that the audience has time to see and absorb what it is you are trying to show them.

The biggest mistake inexperienced presenters make in the handling of visuals is hurrying while demonstrating. Handle each object that you pick up as a mass of weight in space. Slowly move it from the right to the left across your body, then turn it around and repeat this procedure. You may or may not be speaking at the same time, depending on how you plan to handle this. If you are, a description of your object—always prepared in advance—will usually prove suitable. Be sure to have a table or a chair placed near you before you begin, so that you can dispose of your object smoothly when you are done with your demonstration.

If you intend to use handouts, do *not* pass them out during your talk. People will begin to read, and you will lose your audience. If you are using a chart or a graph, use a pointer or a long pencil. Never use your finger or your hand. Always remember to move slowly—*very* slowly.

ELECTRONIC AIDS

In this technological age, use of slides, films, and visual or aural tapes to make a talk or speech more vivid is increasingly common. A series of slides or a short film involve an audience much more deeply in the subject being presented to them. Tape recorders make it possible to discuss certain subjects—a comparison of the singing styles of Maria Callas, Joan Sutherland, and Beverly Sills, for instance—that would otherwise be difficult to tackle. But electronic aids also have their pitfalls and require both a clear understanding of how they should be used and additional preparation so that they are smoothly integrated into the speech as a whole.

To begin with, it must be understood that such materials are wasted and may create confusion unless they are directly tied to a point that is being made verbally. If you are using slides, for example, they should be employed sparingly and only when they are truly pertinent. Otherwise, the audience will quickly become as bored as when they are forced to sit through a half hour of pictures their next door neighbors took during a summer vacation visit to the Grand Canyon. A slide that does not illustrate a specific point has no place in a formal presentation.

Similarly, a five-minute film can greatly increase the impact of a twenty- to thirty-minute speech. But, too often, films are shown to the audience at the wrong time. A film, by its very nature, becomes the automatic high point of a speech. Speakers are often tempted to show a film at the beginning of their talk. This is always a mistake, for several reasons. First, the audience will not fully appreciate or understand the significance of a film if they have not been prepared for its content. What, they will ask themselves, are we supposed to be looking for in this film? What are we supposed to be getting out of it? If a film is shown at the beginning of a talk, the speech that follows is likely to seem anticlimactic. The audience may even become confused as you make reference to parts of the film they didn't understand when it was shown. A film has far greater effect if it is shown at the end of a speech, serving as the speaker's climactic point and followed only by a brief conclusion.

In addition to making certain that an audience is fully prepared for the slides, films, or tapes to be shown, and that these aids serve to drive home specific points, the speaker must also be sure he or she knows how to handle the equipment required. There is nothing more unsettling for an audience than to be shown slides that are out of order or upside down, or to have to wait while a film is rethreaded or while the speaker tries to find the right spot on an aural tape. Careful advance preparation and additional rehearsal time are necessary to insure that all goes as planned.

If you are bringing your own slide projector, film equipment, or tape recorder, you will know how it works. But if such equipment is being provided by the group you are addressing, you should plan to arrive far enough ahead of time so that you have ample time to practice. If someone else is going to be running the slide or film projector, you should spend time explaining what you want beforehand. In addition, the person running a slide projector should always be provided a copy of your speech, with the placement of the slides clearly indicated in bold print. Each slide should be numbered, with the corresponding number appearing in the text of the speech.

Such preparations are essential to a smooth presentation. You should never attempt to use electronic aids unless you have the time to make preparations and to rehearse use of the aids as fully as any other aspect of your talk.

THE DEMONSTRATION TALK (THE HOW-TO)

One of the best ways to develop confidence for a demonstration talk is to do a "how-to test run." The how-to presentation is one of the most popular events of my seminars, because it gives students the opportunity to describe and demonstrate a hobby or a skill that they are deeply involved with and feel very knowledgeable about.

This talk becomes a working model for any other demonstration or teaching presentation you may ever have to give. For example, the ability to explain technical material to nonexperts can be a great asset. The principles of good organization used to simplify a complicated recipe in the how-to presentation later in this chapter can be applied to any technical material. The key is to make the information easy to listen to so that others will be able to understand it and learn from it.

Here is a list of some of the how-to's done by my students and clients:

- How to change a flat
- How to make wine
- How to do tatting
- How to bring up an adolescent
- How to sail a seventy-foot craft
- How to make forty tiny cherry cheese tarts
- How to run an orientation meeting for a group of new salesmen
- How to build a geodesic dome
- How to collect fossils
- How to do an astrological chart
- How to fix up a loft

- How to answer the personal columns so that you can meet eligible bachelors
- How to prepare for a tax audit
- How to set up a food cooperative
- How to service a brokerage client
- How to calculate investment performance results
- How to get stock market information
- How to convert rental property to a cooperative
- How to hunt wild geese
- How to watch a football game

These are just a few of the hundreds of how-to topics that have been presented in my seminars. In all the years that I have been teaching, I have never met a single person who did not have expertise and interest in at least one skill or hobby.

Example of a How-to

Introductory remark: I am particularly addicted to Chinese food. I often find myself sitting in my apartment late at night with a sudden, unrelenting desire for Moo Shu Pork or Beef Chow Fon. Several years ago in order to save my marriage, which was under stress due to my impulsive treks to Chinatown, a friend bought me a wok. Since then I have developed a moderate talent for preparing Chinese dishes.

(Pause)

Topic: Tonight I'm going to talk about how to prepare chicken with vegetables and peanuts, Szechuan style.

(Pause)

Thesis: I believe that preparing delicious Chinese dishes can be easy and fun.

(Pause)

Background: I first became interested in Chinese cooking ten years ago when I roomed with a Chinese-American at college. He would prepare many excellent (and, most important for us in those days, economical) meals in his magic wok. Given my great affinity for Chinese cuisine, and my limited financial resources, I became an attentive student. Also, I noted how useful my friend's skill was in planning romantic evenings. My new culinary skills brought me a popularity on campus that I had never enjoyed before. After college I rarely used my cooking skills until I received the gift of the wok. Now I use my wok at least once a week.

(Pause)

Body/Point Section: In order to ensure that your cooking experience will be enjoyable and as simple as possible, it is very important to have the proper utensils and all ingredients lined up and ready to be used. The actual frying, which is done over very high heat, takes very little time; this is the secret of the fresh flavor and crisp texture of stir-fried cooking. Most of the chef's time is devoted to careful preparation.

The utensils you will need are a wok with a cover, a large pot, wok utensils (a large spoon and a spatula will do), a cutting board, a cleaver or good cutting knife, measuring spoons, a measuring cup, and seven bowls and/or cups to hold ingredients (hold up each utensil).

The following ingredients are needed:

2 chicken cutlets (about one lb.)
2 stalks of scallions
1 clove of garlic
2 red chili peppers (or ¼ teaspoon cayenne pepper)
12 snow pea pods (if unavailable, increase green beans by ¼ cup)
¼ cup of celery, chopped
¼ cup of mushrooms, chopped
¼ cup of onions, chopped
½ cup of bean sprouts (fresh if possible, but canned will do)
½ cup of green beans (or broccoli)
2 teaspoons of cornstarch

$\frac{1}{2}$ cup of strong chicken stock
wedge of fresh ginger (size of a quarter)
$\frac{1}{3}$ cup of shelled peanuts
honey
soy sauce
sesame or corn oil
rice wine or dry sherry

(Pause)

The second step is to prepare all the ingredients, cutting, mixing, and dividing them into seven bowls, ready to cook. Cube the chicken and place it in a bowl. Dice the scallions and the garlic, and halve the chili peppers. Place them together in a small bowl. Mix together the pea pods, celery, mushrooms, onions, bean sprouts, and green beans in a large bowl. Mix the 2 teaspoons of cornstarch with 2 teaspoons of water and 1 teaspoon of honey in a small bowl. Prepare the chicken stock and set aside. Smash the ginger wedge with the spatula (this allows more flavor to escape while it is cooking). Have the peanuts shelled and ready to be added.

Step two is most enjoyable when you give yourself plenty of time to prepare all of the ingredients so that you do not feel rushed or under pressure.

(Pause)

The third step, cooking the vegetables, should be timed with split-second precision. This is much easier than it sounds. Heat the wok (moderately high) with 1 tablespoon of oil. Add the wedge of ginger and 1 teaspoon of soy sauce. Fry for 15 seconds. Add the vegetables (pea-pod and green-bean mixture) and cook for 30 seconds. Add the stock, cover, and cook for 2 minutes. Remove the vegetables and stock to the pot.

Now you are ready to cook the chicken. Reheat the wok with 1 tablespoon of oil. Add 1 teaspoon of soy sauce and the scallion-garlic-pepper mixture. Cook for 15 seconds. Add 1 tablespoon of sherry or rice wine and the chicken and cook for 2 minutes. Then add the peanuts and cook for 15 seconds. Add the vegetables and cook until the vegetables are hot. Add the cornstarch solution, which will thicken the gravy.

Once the gravy has reached a thick but liquid consistency, the dish is ready.

(Pause)

Serving such a culinary masterpiece always fills me with pleasure. I like to bring it to the table as soon as it is ready, although it reheats easily without any loss of flavor. Serve it with rice (I prefer the brown variety) and beer or a light white wine (not too sweet). Whatever beverage you choose, make sure that you have large quantities of it on hand, or lots of cold water, as this is a spicy meal. We have found that a light tangy dessert, such as citrus fruit or sherbert, is the best following act for this entrée. But no matter what you serve with this dish, it is so delicious and complete that it can stand by itself as a good meal.

(Pause)

In conclusion, let me urge all of you to learn the joys of Chinese cooking. There are many dishes as delicious and easy to prepare as chicken and vegetables and peanuts. All you need is a wok, a few leisure hours, and a well-developed appetite for Chinese food.

The next exercise involves a how-to presentation. Read the instructions carefully, and then organize your own how-to. The purpose of this exercise is to give you an opportunity to practice and develop skill in the use of visuals and to teach you the principles for presenting technical material. Once you have put together a how-to using a hobby, skill, or professional procedure you are familiar with, you will see how relatively easy it is to put together any talk that involves demonstrating a work-related project.

Exercise Twenty-four: The How-to Talk

1. Select a hobby or skill that you know well and would like to talk about. (If you are stuck, you can always use the preparation of a favorite dish.)

2. Now write a complete seven-minute talk, using the Action Formula model. As with previous speeches, your how-to will have: an *introduction,* a *topic sentence,* a *thesis sentence,* a *background section,* a *point section* with several subheadings, a *climax,* and a *conclusion.* You will see how well this structure lends itself to a demonstration.

3. Assemble your visual aids—from one to four should be enough—and decide where you are going to use them. Usually visuals are employed in the point section. If you only have one visual, the climax might be a good place to put it.

4. Arrange your visuals at the place where you are going to give your talk.

5. Now go through a complete rehearsal of your talk.

Rehearsal

- Sit in your chair. Center yourself.
- With your cards in your lap, concentrate on the tingling in your fingertips.
- Take your cards in your hand and *very slowly* pull yourself up to your feet.
- Stand in place and balance your weight evenly on both feet.
- Walk slowly and naturally up to the front of your imaginary audience, concentrating on your fingertips as you move.
- *Slowly* turn and face your imaginary audience, keeping your arms at your sides.
- Run through your checklist: My head feels . . .
My eyes are . . .
My mouth is . . .
My shoulders are . . .

My neck is . . .
My chest feels . . .
My heart is . . .
My arms are . . .
My stomach is . . .
My hands feel . . .
My legs feel . . .
My knees are . . .
The bottom of my
feet are . . .

- Now begin your introductory without reading from your cards. When you come to your background section, you may read from your cards, but look at your audience from time to time.
- Go through your entire speech remembering the instructions given in this chapter for the slow, precise handling of all visual material. Sections of your speech that involve the use of visuals should be familiar enough to you so that you do not have to read from your cards. (You may need both hands free in order to demonstrate an object or a technique, and in the case of slides or film the hall will be darkened.)

Progress Report

Date	Time	Strong Spot	Weak Spot	Comment	Calm–Nervous (1–10)

CHAPTER 11

Taking Questions from the Floor

Over the years I have found there are two main points of view concerning the questions a speaker is asked after he has finished his regular talk.

Most people dread being put in this situation. Jay S., a staff psychologist with a municipal hospital, had been avoiding making presentations because, as he said, "I'm terrified of anyone asking me a question I will not be able to answer. I feel as if I will be exposed and that everyone will realize how little I really do know."

The other point of view, certainly one that is in the minority, was expressed by Barbara H., an account executive with a pharmaceutical company. "I love the question and answer part, because as soon as I relate directly to another person I feel better."

Both of these perspectives are essentially wrong, because they do not approach the issue of questions from the floor in terms of purpose.

The purpose of taking questions from the floor is primarily to add variety to the presentation by giving the audience a limited opportunity to participate. In responding, your objective is to present yourself and your point of view as calmly, smoothly, and credibly as possible.

Since you are in charge of your presentation, you make the rules concerning the question and answer period. Keep the following points in mind:

1. Call on as many different questioners as possible.
2. Limit each member of the audience to one question.
3. Keep your answers brief, so that you have time to call on other questioners. You don't have to tell everything you know in answer to a question. Pick one thing you wish to emphasize and say it.
4. Do not get into a discussion with a member of the audience. If you do, the rest of the audience will feel left out, and the discussion will become a personal conversation in public.
5. Above all, do not allow the audience to challenge or debate you or to use the question period as an opportunity to confront you with embarrassing questions or inquiries. Your job is to be as informative as possible, clarifying points or giving requested information, not to engage in debate. Many speakers are thrown off balance when a member of the audience tries to debate with them, often feeling compelled to defend or explain their positions. As soon as you start defending yourself, however, you lose psychological ground.

A politician who was one of my clients put this matter in sharp perspective. "When Roosevelt was Secretary of the Navy," he pointed out, "they used to say that he was like a goose-down pillow. The harder you hit him, the more he fluffed up." That should be the tactic of any speaker in a question and answer session.

But how can you avoid defending yourself?

To begin with, you must understand the rules of the game. Confrontational or embarrassing questions are seldom accidental. The purpose of the questioner is to throw you off guard, to upset you. If you come back with a knee-jerk defense, giving your answer too quickly, you will have fallen into a trap that you may have great difficulty getting out of.

The proper procedure for answering questions is always to wait for three seconds (you can count off the time and maintain control over your bodily responses by tapping slowly with your fingertips against your leg or the podium itself) and then *repeat the question to the entire audience.*

> *Question:* How long do you think it will take before we can complete this project?
> *Answer: (To the entire group you say)* The question is, How long will it take before we can complete the project?

There are several reasons why you should always repeat a question:

1. It gives you time to think.
2. It assures that everyone in the audience has a chance to hear the question.
3. It keeps you from being put in a position where you engage in personal dialogue with one member of the group while the audience is observing you, as this invariably turns into a power struggle and may cost you your position as leader.
4. It keeps the attention of the audience on you, not on the person who asked the question. When you repeat the question you take it away from the person who asked it and make it your own, thus pulling the attention of the audience back to you. Also, by repeating the question with your own inflection, you take the bite out of any attack.

THE UNANSWERABLE QUESTION

Invariably one of my students will ask, "What if you really do not know the answer to a question?"

Although it is most worthy and honorable simply to say, "I don't know," when indeed you do not know, the only people who seem able to do this with confidence and aplomb are specialists and experts. For the beginning speaker, or the nervous speaker suffering from low self-esteem, to make a public confession of ignorance is a damnable humiliation; and such humiliation is what many people dread most.

Remember the purpose of your presentation. Your objective is to present yourself and your point of view as calmly, smoothly, and credibly as possible. Your goal in the question and answer period is to hold on to your position as the leader of the group. If you are going to be upset or worried about having to say, "I don't know," don't say it.

Instead say:

- "That is a very interesting question. As a matter of fact, we are in the midst of gathering that information, and I will be glad to get it to you as soon as I have it."
- "I would like to check my figures very carefully before I rattle them off here. I will be glad to send you a memo when I get back to my office."
- "That information is not available at the present time."

Another good strategy for taking you out of the combat zone is to reply to an inflammatory remark with apparent sympathy. For example, you can say, "Now that is a very interesting piece of information," and then add a different piece of information that you would prefer your audience to remember.

Last year one of my clients, a public figure, was interviewed on the radio and responded with great defensiveness to many of the questions. We later discussed the interview, and I suggested a more strategic way of handling this kind of frontal attack.

Much to my delight, at his next news conference, when a reporter said, "Do you mean to suggest that this is a scandal being uncovered?" my client replied, "I can see that you are quite concerned. I too am quite concerned and appreciate your interest." This response totally caught the reporter off guard and served to defuse the inflammatory tone of the encounter.

Sometimes a questioner will challenge you by making what amounts to a speech of his own. When a question becomes a long dissertation, what is happening is that a member of the audience is trying to take over your leadership role. By all means interrupt. Don't wait for the speaker to finish. Count to three and *force yourself to say,* "Would you be so kind as to ask your question."

If the questioner persists in monopolizing the floor, count to three, interrupt again, and say, "Thank you for your contribution. May I have the next question."

Most members of the audience will be delighted by your response. They too resent moves made to unseat the speaker. The longer you allow a member of the audience to monopolize attention, the more impatient the audience will be for you to reassert control. Remember, this is your time on stage. You have the right to interrupt any person who tries to take the audience's attention away from you.

You do *not* necessarily have to answer the exact question that has been asked. I once heard best-selling novelist Gore Vidal discuss his technique for dealing with the questions of talk show hosts. "You have to make up your mind before you go on that you are going to make the following points. Don't make too many points because they can't remember them. . . . It doesn't make any difference what they ask, you just go right on—'Yes, that's interesting'—and go right on to the point you were going to make. It's like any other kind of skill. You have to learn how to do it."

You too can shape your response in terms of whatever information you want to communicate. Furthermore, many possible questions can be anticipated. There is no better way to ensure smooth performance in a question and answer session than to prepare answers for ten questions that you think may possibly be asked. Write out your answers so that they focus on *what you want to say.*

Exercise Twenty-five: Rehearsing Your Answers

1. Review your talk and make a list of ten possible questions you may be asked.
2. Now go over your talk and pick out ten pieces of information that might be used to answer these questions.

There is nothing wrong with repeating information during a question and answer period. In fact, one of the best ways to deal with a hostile questioner is to repeat his question and then say, "As I have already pointed out. . . ." This approach, with its suggestion that the questioner wasn't listening closely enough, serves to enhance your position and to put the questioner on the defensive.

3. Write out the answers to the possible questions and rehearse them. You can have a friend or spouse feed you the questions, or you can use a tape recorder.

During an actual question and answer period, it is always best to give a rehearsed answer if that is at all possible. Many people feel that they are cheating when they give a prepared answer. They think it neither fair nor spontaneous to do so and that they must think on their feet at any cost. However, the cost is likely to be high. Answers given off the top of the head often get a speaker into trouble. The professional speaker always has a set of rehearsed answers. Before any presidential news conference, White House aides spend long hours preparing briefing books full of possible questions and appropriate answers that the President can thoroughly rehearse before appearing before the press. *Public speaking is a public performance,* as every politician, official representative, or statesman knows only too well. When you get up to speak, you are representing yourself, and it is in your best interest to plan ahead and prepare ahead, to rehearse exactly what you intend to say.

HOW TO HAVE ALL THE ANSWERS

Studies have shown that in some cases the fear of public speaking may be connected to a fear of humiliation as a result of a public confrontation the speaker believes he cannot handle.

Richard B. spent a good deal of his time figuring out strategies to avoid making public presentations because he dreaded the thought that he might be asked questions that would prove to be too difficult for him to handle when he was on the spot in front of an audience.

During a private consultation, when I asked him what it was that he was afraid of being asked, he became extremely uncomfortable. He said he could not think clearly enough to come up with anything specific. He just felt overwhelmed with dread.

Realizing that this client needed a more directive approach, I said, "Supposing you could have complete control over all the questions that you might be asked? What is the one question that you would not let anyone ask you?" Richard replied, "I certainly would not want them to ask me how far over budget we are." The problem now was to sit down and try to work out an answer to this possible question beforehand, an answer that would make reasonable sense to a critical audience. To do so, Richard contacted a colleague and asked for help in figuring out an answer he could reasonably respond with. Once he had identified the *specific* source of his dread, he was able to overcome it by fully preparing beforehand for the anticipated attack.

If you have been concerned about your inability to deal with potentially embarrassing questions, the list below will offer you a selection of possible booby traps. When are preparing your presentation, look at this list, and if one or two happen to hit home, try to formulate relevant questions that may possibly be asked. Then *write out* brief but satisfactory responses and rehearse them along with your presentation. When later you hear a potential killer question being asked, you will be able to reply confidently, "I knew you would ask that question and I just happen to have the answer."

- What question do you hope you will not be asked?

  ____

- What question may prove embarrassing to you?

  ____

- What question do you know you do not have the answer to?

  ____

- What question refers to your weakest point?

  ____

- What question will bring up a past error or omission?

  ____

You should also make up a list of questions you would *like* to be asked.

The following questions may not be asked directly, but you certainly should be able to fit the answers to one or two of them into your response to another question. Formulate several of the following suggestions into specific questions and then *write out* triumphant answers. Rehearse these along with your presentation, the chances are good that you will be able to make use of them.

- What question would you love to be asked?

  ____

- What question will show you off to best advantage?

  ____

- What question refers to your strongest point?

  ____

- What question would you ask yourself after listening to your talk?

  ____

- What question refers to a past triumph?

  ____

Thoroughly preparing yourself beforehand to deal with unwanted questions and having especially strong answers to questions you would like to be asked will make it possible for you to look good no matter what the circumstances. Even when a speaker does not have all the answers, if he is able to respond smoothly and confidently, the audience will come away with a good impression. Remember: **looking and sounding good is as important as having all the answers.**

THE ABUSIVE QUESTION OR REMARK

When speaking in a public forum one cannot have control over who will be there or over what questions and remarks will be made. It may happen that you will be challenged by a very aggressive or argumentative member of the audience, perhaps someone who is not totally "responsible" for what he or she is saying.

Even if you as the speaker are the recipient of an insulting or abusive question, the fact remains that you are in full visibility, and how you handle the situation will affect the way your audience views your presentation.

In the case of an abusive questioner, the very best strategy to adopt either in a public forum or on a debating panel is never to try reasoning logically with your antagonist. A verbal assault cannot hit you if you refuse to participate in the give and take of such an exchange.

What can you do?

First let us discuss the strategy, then we will look at an example.

When any verbal abuse is forthcoming—whether in insulting references to you personally or to your profession or group, or in accusations as to your integrity or the integrity of your group, or in references intended to humiliate you or your group—the following strategy is recommended:

1. Define who you are.
2. Define your purpose in making the presentation.
3. Explicitly refuse to enter into any personal debate—and stick to your refusal.
4. Focus your attention on the audience—not on your antagonist.

Here is an example of an excellent response, given by a Talk-Power client, a psychiatrist, during a presentation in a public forum. (A member of the audience asked her an insinuating question in reference to her fees.)

> I am a trained professional with many years of experience. *(defining her role)*
>
> I am here to share with my audience information and my point of view about the issue. *(defining her purpose in being there)*
>
> I am not here to enter into personal debate with members of the audience. Next question . . .

Perhaps you feel that if you were the recipient of an abusive remark you would be too nervous to handle the situation with the same kind of aplomb. In that case, additional work may be necessary to insure that you will be in command during a question and answer period. The following Sense-Memory Imaging Rehearsal, based on a combination of acting techniques and behavioral training methods, can be helpful to even the most ill-at-ease speaker.

Exercise Twenty-six: The Sense-Memory Imaging Rehearsal for Questions from the Floor

1. After you have completed and rehearsed your talk, make a list of ten questions, wanted or unwanted, that you think you may be asked, and write out *a strong but brief* answer for each question (preferably *less* than 75 words).
2. Sit in your chair. Close your eyes. Center yourself.
3. Take twenty inhalations and exhalations, breathing in through your nostrils, blowing out through your lips, and counting each inhalation and exhalation.
4. Imagine that you have given your talk. Try to see the room you are in. What kind of light is there in the room? Feel yourself sitting in the particular chair that you will be sitting in or standing where you will be standing.
5. Try to visualize what you are wearing. Visualize who is sitting next to you . . . any other people in the room.
6. If there is any particular sound in the room, try to hear it. Take your time to *get the feel* of the experience.
7. Now imagine that you are being asked a question. Visualize who is asking the question. Try to hear it being asked. Pause. Imagine that you are repeating the question, and then answer the question, taking your time to do so. Imagine yourself answering the question as intelligently as you possibly can. Hear the murmur of approval from your audience.
8. Feel the pleasant vibes you are getting as result of your excellent response, and go onto the next question. Visualize who is asking the question, what he or she is wearing. Pause. Imagine that you are repeating the question and then answer the question, once again with thoughtful intelligence. Again, visualize the approving

faces of your audience and allow yourself to bask in the pleasant feelings of your success.

9. Continue in this manner until there are no longer any questions forthcoming in your imaging. Remember to imagine yourself answering each question thoughtfully and well, and your audience receiving each answer with approval and interest. Do *not* under any circumstances allow yourself any imaging that is disapproving or hostile to you. If however, a negative image does come up, simply imagine yourself erasing the image from your mind with a huge eraser, and go on to the next question.

The rules of this exercise do not allow for any disapproving responses from your audience. If you find it impossible to do your imaging without these negative images, then you are following an extremely self-defeating pattern of behavior that you need to work on. In that case, put your entire visualization on tape. Simply repeat aloud the instructions above. Voice your questions on the tape recorder and give yourself enough time to answer the question. Follow the instructions for imaging an approving response, and do that imaging aloud. Then go on to the next question. It will be much easier for you to follow the taped, spoken instructions than to try to imagine the approval if that is particularly difficult for you.

Tape Recorder Instructions

Record the following message on your tape recorder, speaking slowly and distinctly. Pause for two seconds wherever dots appear in the text.

> I am sitting in my chair. . . . . . . My eyes are closed. . . . . . . I am now centering my body . . . . . . focusing inward . . . . . . sensing that my body is perfectly balanced between

my right and left buttock. . . . . . . My head is centered between my right and left shoulder. . . . . . . My stomach is relaxed. . . . . . . I will now take twenty inhalations and exhalations, breathing in through my nose and exhaling through my mouth and counting as I do this. . . . . . . (NOTE: *When you make your original tape, take the time to breathe twenty inhalations and exhalations so that the proper amount of time is accounted for on your tape.*)

I am now imagining that I have just given my presentation and have asked for questions from the floor. . . . . . . I am standing or sitting where I would be in this situation. . . . . . . I see the room I am in. . . . . . . I am trying to see the particular light that is in that room. . . . . . . I see the clothes that I am wearing. . . . . . . I look down, and I can see my shoes or my boots. . . . . . . I see the people who are in the room with me. . . . . . . I see several people individually. . . . . . . I see what they are wearing. . . . . . . I try to hear any kind of sound that is in the room or outside of this room. . . . . . . I am breathing comfortably. . . . . . . I feel pleasantly excited. . . . . . . Now I am imagining that the first question is being asked. . . . . . .

(Fill in here with your question.)

I see the person who is asking the question. . . . . . . I am breathing calmly. . . . . . . I am now repeating the question out loud. . . . . . . *(Repeat the question aloud. Pause. Give your answer.)* . . . . . . My answer is exactly what I would have wanted to say. . . . . . . I am pleased at how well it came out. . . . . . . I can hear the murmur of approval from my audience. . . . . . . I can see them nodding in my direction. . . . . . . I feel the pleasant vibes that I am getting from my excellent response. . . . . . . I now hear the next question. . . . . . .

(Put the next question on the tape here.)

I see who is asking this question. . . . . . . I am breathing calmly. . . . . . . I am repeating the question out loud. . . . . . *(Repeat the question aloud.)* . . . . . . I am now answering the question with thoughtful intelligence. . . . . . . *(Answer out loud.)* . . . . . . Once again I am pleased with my answer. . . . . . . I see the approving faces of my audience looking at me. . . . . . . I feel that I have been accepted and understood. . . . . . . I am basking in a feeling of success.

Continue in this manner asking your questions . . . . . . breathing . . . . . . repeating your questions . . . . . . answering your question . . . . . . and noting approving responses to your answer from the audience until you have gone through all of your questions.

CHAPTER 12

The Public Speaker's Bill of Rights

In the preceding chapters we have focused on behavioral techniques to help the fearful public speaker develop the performance skills and organizational speechwriting skills necessary for overcoming public-speaking phobia. However, while a lack of performance or speechwriting skills in themselves can and do cause people to tremble at the very thought of speaking in public, there is often another element involved. This third element is *lack of assertiveness.*

Many people who have been raised in a highly manipulated environment have difficulty asserting themselves, finding it very hard to take a position, then to express that position and hold onto it. Individuals who, when growing up, were not allowed to express an opinion or point of view that differed from the opinions of parents, teachers, or peers invariably encounter great difficulty when it comes to standing up before a group and presenting a point of view.

Do you have an assertiveness problem? To find out, take the following test.

Assertiveness Test

Do I believe that . . .	Yes	No	Unsure
1. I have the *right* to express myself?			
2. I have the *right* to my own point of view?			
3. I have the *right* to ask others to listen?			
4. I have the *right* to inform or teach others?			
5. I have the *right* to try?			
6. I have the *right* to grow?			
7. I have the *right* to achieve?			
8. I have the *right* to make a mistake?			
9. I have the *right* to fail if I try?			
10. I have the *right* to try again?			
11. I have the *right* to feel anxious and uncomfortable at first?			
12. I have the *right* not to know "everything"?			
13. I have the *right* to stand in front of a group?			

14. I have the *right* to be a leader?

15. I have the *right* to my speech time?

16. Others have the *right* to their point of view?

17. Others have the *right* to disagree with me?

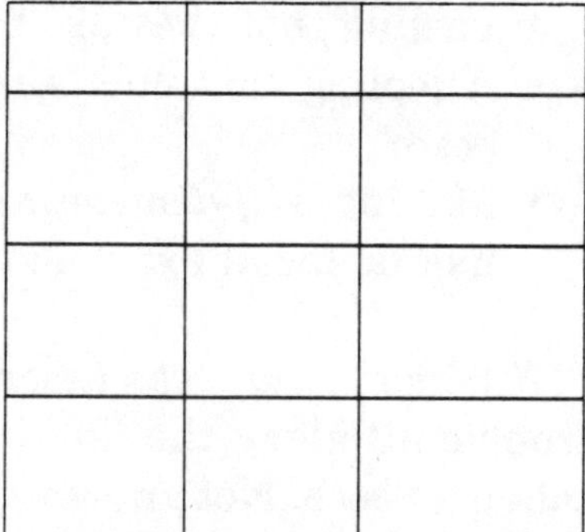

If you answered no to a number of these questions, you are not alone. In the seminars and classes I have run over the past several years, I have found the results of this test to be astonishingly negative in many areas. For example:

- 50 percent have felt that they did not have the right to express themselves.
- 65 percent have felt that they lacked the right not to know everything.
- 40 percent have felt that they did not have the right to ask others to listen.
- 60 percent have believed that they lacked the right to make a mistake.

Obviously, individuals who do not feel they have the right to express themselves or who do not feel they have the right to make a mistake are likely to be terrified of speaking in public. In a presentational situation, their responses may include:

- Not knowing *what* they think about an important issue
- Thinking several *contradictory* things
- Feeling sure that they are thinking the *wrong* thing

- Feeling that they are being *criticized* or *condemned*
- A feeling that one is really a fraud and will be *exposed*
- Making *self-demeaning* and *self-derogatory* statements, facial expressions, or gestures

A person who lacks assertiveness is likely to run into trouble all along the line in preparing and delivering a talk or speech. Not knowing quite what to think about an issue, or thinking contradictory things, such a person is bound to find it hard to develop a clear thesis or to support it with telling points. During the actual presentation, the fear of being thought a fraud or of being criticized will contribute to the lack of control over physical reactions to stress that afflict so many inexperienced public speakers. Trying to protect himself, the speaker may well make self-demeaning statements that undermine his credibility altogether—"You may not find this interesting, but . . ."; "You probably have heard this story before"; "I didn't really have much time to prepare this report."

It is important to recognize that the apologetic, nonassertive person has actually been *trained*—by parents, teachers, and peers—to avoid taking positions that are at variance with what he or she has been told to believe. What begins as the admonitions of parents, teachers, or friends eventually becomes internalized, so that the individual becomes governed by a complex invisible police state in his own head that denies the right to self-expression.

How can one break out of such self-defeating patterns of behavior? How can one learn new, more self-accepting responses and develop more satisfying attitudes—attitudes that will more closely express the individual's true feelings and point of view in a socially appropriate manner?

Let's begin by establishing a Public Speaker's Bill of Rights. If you answered every question on the test at the beginning of this chapter with a *yes,* then you have already adopted such a bill of rights for yourself. But most of you have probably answered some of those questions *no.* Let's turn the questions into statements and look at them more closely.

The Public Speaker's Bill of Rights

1. I have the *right* to express myself.
2. I have the *right* to my own point of view.
3. I have the *right* to ask others to listen.
4. I have the *right* to inform or teach others.
5. I have the *right* to try.
6. I have the *right* to grow.
7. I have the *right* to achieve.
8. I have the *right* to make a mistake.
9. I have the *right* to fail if I try.
10. I have the *right* to try again.
11. I have the *right* to feel anxious and uncomfortable at first.
12. I have the *right* not to know "everything."
13. I have the *right* to stand in front of a group.
14. I have the *right* to be a leader.
15. I have the *right* to my speech time.
16. Others have the *right* to their point of view.
17. Others have the *right* to disagree with me.

If you have doubts or misgivings concerning your rights in any one of these areas, those doubts will affect your ability to present a confident and convincing speech. These doubts are actual programmed messages that play over and over again in your head and inhibit you from successfully speaking in public. The value of the Public Speaker's Bill of Rights is that it makes it possible for you to zero in on the *particular* area in which you are denying yourself the right to express yourself freely. Many people who fear speaking in public will readily admit that they "lack confidence" or are "afraid to speak out." But these are vague generalities, akin to telling the family physician that you "don't feel very well." Before you can find a remedy, the exact nature of the problem must be pinpointed.

Jane S., one of my students, felt that she had to know everything there was to know about a subject before she could make a speech. As a result, Jane tormented herself with doubts and apprehensions about her qualifications for doing a presentation. Keeping a low profile in her career, she missed out on countless opportunities to demonstrate the considerable level of expertise she did in fact possess.

It was not until she began analyzing her reactions to the Public Speaker's Bill of Rights that Jane realized where the problem lay and understood how thoroughly she had denied herself the right not to know "everything." With this insight, she began to develop a new perspective. The truth of the matter is that no one really knows "everything" about anything. That is impossible. Even if one did know everything, it would be impossible to communicate it all to an audience in a speech. Even her boss, Jane recalled, had given a talk a short while earlier in which he had offhandedly admitted he didn't know the answer to a question.

Now in preparing a speech, Jane catches herself when she starts worrying that she does not have all the facts. She repeats to herself, "I have the right not to know everything." And then she adds, "I have the right to make a mistake"; "I have the right to fail"; "I have the right to try again."

By reexamining the self-defeating denial of her rights as a speaker, she has been able to substitute self-affirming, helpful messages to herself, which, combined with her newly acquired speaking skills, make it possible for her to make presentations with increasing comfort and confidence.

Some people report that repeating self-affirming messages to themselves, whether silently or out loud, is not enough to overcome the deeply ingrained inhibitions of a lifetime of doubt. For such people I recommend a simple procedure.

- Choose three or four rights that you have particular difficulty asserting, and write them out on 5 × 8 cards.
- Put those cards up around your apartment. If you don't want them in plain sight, attach them to the inside of your dresser drawers, of the refrigerator, of the bathroom cabinet, or of other places where you will see them regularly. Each time you notice one of the signs, repeat the message silently to yourself. "I have the right to make a mistake," or "I have the right to express myself."

These regular reminders of your rights will gradually help you get rid of old self-defeating ideas and replace them with new self-affirming messages.

TALK-POWER FOR WOMEN

I have found that women often find it especially difficult to assert their right to speak. In an article for the Sunday *New York Times* (March 22, 1981), Colette Dowling writes about her book *The Cinderella Complex,* which takes note of this problem.

In a survey of 200 students training to become psychoanalysts at the William Alanson White Institute in New York, Ruth Moulton, a senior training analyst there (she is also on the faculty of Columbia University) found that 50 percent of the women tested were unable to speak in public, as compared with 20 percent of the men. For some women, the anxiety was so overwhelming it produced attacks of dizziness and fainting. In trying to state their positions, some women become confused, forget what they wanted to say, can't find the right word, can't look people in the eye. Or they blush, stutter or find that their voices quiver the minute someone disagrees with them.

These findings corroborate my own observations. In the area of public speaking women have the same difficulties as men *plus* . . .

The reasons for that plus are several.

- Many women traditionally have been overprotected and infantalized. Thus it is especially difficult for them to take on the adult role of leadership.
- There may be a handicap in that, at times, women as well as men feel that a woman must prove herself.
- Women have been socialized with conditioned "feminine gestures" that are not compatible with credibility. Examples of this are head bobbing, looking around for approval, touching the hair and body, and smiling excessively and giggling.
- Many women do not know how to dress professionally for maximum effect.
- Women rarely see feminine role models who are appropriate examples of leadership and presentation.
- Many women are not clear about the difference between assertive, aggressive, and cutesy compliant behavior in a leadership role.

- High visibility is often extremely anxiety-provoking for women.
- Women are very critical of one another—more so than men are—and do not trust other women as much as they do men. As a result, women tend to be overly self-critical and not trust their own abilities.

The reasons for lack of confidence and the high degree of public speaking dysfunction among women will come as no surprise. The point to be made, however, is that they involve *learned* behaviors considered appropriate to the "feminine role."

Learned behaviors can always be modified and more desirable behaviors substituted in their place. Follow-up studies of women who have completed the Talk-Power program show that because of the proven behavior modification techniques used to concentrate upon body awareness (sense of self) and to develop skills for systematic organization of thought and techniques for coping with anxiety, a general increase of confidence in all areas occurs.

One of my clients, a very talented and energetic woman, had been vice president of a civic organization for several years. She was the only female member of this important organization, made up of 125 of the eastern seaboard's most powerful corporate executives and chairmen of the board. She had declined the opportunity to run for the organization's presidency, even though she longed for the status and prestige this office would give her. Her mouth would become dry, her heartbeat would accelerate and she would lose her breath whenever she tried to talk. She learned to accept a role of leadership in this mostly male setting by using her Public Speaker's Bill of Rights. She learned to concentrate upon her physical reactions through the simple exercises she practiced. These basic techniques helped her control her anxiety so that eventually she became an excellent speaker with great personal charm. Today she enjoys the position of being one of the only women presidents of this kind of civic organization in the United States. It is a position she calls "a dream come true."

The Public Speaker's Bill of Rights is a particularly effective instrument for change because it promotes a consciousness-raising climate. It gives those who suffer a fear of public speaking because of low self-esteem the permission necessary for confident self-expression. It is particularly helpful for women.

Exercise Twenty-seven: Reaffirming Your Rights

Go through the Public Speaker's Bill of Rights and copy down on a separate card any of the rights you have found it difficult to assert in the past. Each time you rehearse a speech, read the list through carefully before you begin. Give yourself permission to speak.

This is not merely a matter of "positive thinking." The explicit repetition of rights that you have failed to assert in the past is a behavioral training technique. Carried out systematically, that repetition will help you change the way you think about yourself as a speaker—indeed, as a person.

CHAPTER 13

Schedules for Busy People

Your speech is your personal production. Anything that begins as an idea and makes its appearance in the world as a finished product goes through a process of production. And as any good manager can tell you, the most successful productions are envisioned, planned, and scheduled with explicit goals, records, budgets, and deadlines.

Since your presentation is a production, your management skills are vitally important to its success.

TALK-POWER PRODUCTION SCHEDULES

Talk-Power schedules fall into two categories.

One type of schedule is for the brief talk (from five to fifteen minutes) that requires little or no research because you are so familiar with the subject.

The second type is for the more demanding assignment. This involves a talk of any length that requires research, investigation, and perhaps the organization of visuals (making transparencies, selecting slides or other materials, etc.).

For the brief talk that requires little or no research, one or two sittings using the game plan that follows as your organizing model should do the trick for the writing of the presentation. Then I recommend at least one week of two complete run-throughs each day for this assignment.

However, the presentation that requires extensive research is a production that must be carefully planned, written, and rehearsed. There is simply no way around it. I have found, however, that most of my students and clients do not have any real grasp on how to go about organizing the time and effort it takes to prepare a complex professional presentation. People are very busy; there are so many other more important things to do. Procrastination leads to avoidance, and before you know it, it is one or two days before your talk and you are frantic, up all night trying to pull something together that will make sense. This approach is, of course, a losing strategy.

A new client, a young lawyer specializing in real estate law, contacted my office for an emergency consultation the very day before he was to appear on TV for a five-minute presentation. Not only was he nervous, but he knew that there were going to be three other panelists, one of whom was highly critical of his position. We hurriedly scheduled a meeting.

When I asked him to go over what it was that he intended to say, he replied in a rather furtive manner, "Well . . . I don't know exactly what I am going to say. You see, I want it to be spontaneous . . . when I get there I will know what I want to say. I don't want to spoil the spontaneity of it all. I have my notes here, and I have to go over them."

It took us three hours to figure out what it was he wanted to say in this five-minute presentation. It took three hours to pinpoint what he would say so as to be on target and to the point, so that he would come across as a professional who really knew his business and was on top of things.

Of course we did the very best that we could. His presentation went as well as it might have under the circumstances, but what a dangerous way to live! It would have made more sense if he had begun to work on his presentation at least a week ahead of time, so that the misery and fright that built up in him could have been avoided. Didn't he deserve to give himself the time it would have taken to use this opportunity to show himself off to best advantage?

When people tell me they work best under pressure, I reply that it is impossible to plan, write, and rehearse a well thought-out presentation one or two days before your scheduled appearance. A hurriedly knocked together talk is a big mistake, especially for people who have a problem with speaking in public in the first place. That mistake is compounded by the fact that many people suffer from *anticipatory anxiety,* a severe form of distress, for days or even weeks before a presentation. It may take the form of sleepless nights, constant worry, and dread that the presentation will turn out to be a disaster.

As many studies have shown, anticipatory anxiety is usually associated with avoidance behavior. A person fearing a task will put off working on it until the last minute. As a deadline draws closer and closer, the anxiety and avoidance both increase. *The best way to begin overcoming anticipatory anxiety is to get to work immediately.*

On the following pages you fill find various charts and rehearsal schedules to help you plan, write, and rehearse your presentations. Copy them and use them each time you have to do a talk.

The Talk-Power Game Plan

The Talk-Power Game Plan has proven invaluable for mapping out your basic organizational work on one or two pages.

Step 1

Whenever you have to do a presentation, fill in all of Part A below *before* you begin to write your talk.

<u>Part A</u>

Type of assignment ________________________
Date assignment received ____________________
Date assignment due ________________________
Number of preparation days __________________
Place ____________________________________
Who will be present ________________________
Topic ____________________________________
Intention *(I would like my audience to . . .)* ________
____
Number of minutes for speech———

Step 2

Now you can begin to write your talk on your 5 × 8 cards.

Whenever you have completed a section, fill in the appropriate information in Part B of the Game Plan. (Remember, the Game Plan is no substitute for your speech. It is simply an overview or map of where you are going.)

Part B

Type of Introduction ______________________________
Topic Sentence ______________________________
Thesis ______________________________
Type of Background ______________________________
Point Section *(Fill in as many as the number of points you intend to use.)*
Point A ______________________________
Point B ______________________________
Point C ______________________________
Point D ______________________________
Climax ______________________________
____
Type of Conclusion ______________________________
____
Choice of visuals (if any) ______________________________
____

Look at your intention again and review your thesis sentence. *Did you do what you set out to do?* (Yes) (No)

A Production Schedule

The following schedule is a model that will illustrate what a two-part writing and rehearsal schedule for a complex presentation can look like.

John H., a public relations account executive, organized this calendar for a very important presentation with a new account. The purpose of his schedule is to show a calendar breakdown of daily writing assignments for a difficult thirty-minute presentation to be given in two weeks.

A Two-Part "Production" Schedule (Sample)

Part 1—Writing Schedule

Day	Assignment	Scheduled Time	Place	Comment for the Next Day's Work (to be filled out at the end of each day's work)
1	Construct calendar for twelve-day work plan. Think about what intro to use.	8–9 AM	Office	Decide on intro—joke, story, or just begin with the topic sentence?
2	Do the intro, topic, and thesis and brainstorm possible points.	Lunch hour	At desk	Work in company library.
3	Do background (corporate) and outline four major points of presentation.	Allow full evening.	Company library	Organize facts and figures in the various points.
4	Complete two points. Order visuals.	8–10 PM	Home	Two points left for the next session. Doublecheck visuals order has gone through.
5	No time to work on the presentation.			
6	Complete last two points. Do conclusion plus one read-through.	1st part 1–2:15 PM Read-through 8–8:30 PM	On plane trip In hotel	Remember to work on question and answer sheet.
7	Prepare question and answer sheet. Work visuals into talk.	8–10 PM	Home	Begin formal rehearsal.

Part 2—Rehearsal Schedule

Day	Start–Finish	Actual Work Done	Comment	Self-Rating—calm–nervous (1–10)
8	8–9 PM	One complete run-through, plus last-minute adjustments with visuals	Need to slow down during the background.	7
9	12–1:45 PM	Two complete rehearsals, plus question and answer section	Beginning to feel a bit better. Need to remember to repeat my questions to audience.	5
10	9–10:30 PM	Two complete rehearsals, plus question and answer section	Things seem to be under control. Still feel nervous, though.	4
11	8:30–10 PM	Trial run two times, once alone, once for wife with questions and answers	Seem to be OK. Still nervous.	4
12	8–9 AM	*DAY OF PRESENTATION* Last run-through with questions and answers	This is it.	5

A Two-Part "Production" Schedule (Model)

Part 1—Writing Schedule

(Use this schedule as a model calendar to structure your time for the written part of your presentation.)

Assignment ______________________ Actual date of presentation ____________

Time ________ Place ________________ Topic ______________________

Intention ______________ Number of minutes talk will take ______________

Day	Scheduled Time	Place	Actual Work Done	Comment for Next Day's Work (to be filled out at the end of each day's work)
1				
2				
3				
4				
5				
6				
7				
8				

Part 2—continued

Day	Time Start–Finish	Weak Spot	Strong Spot	Comment	Self-Rating—calm–nervous 1–10
8					
9					
10					
11					
12					
13					
14					

Day and date of actual presentation: ______________________________

Progress Report

Week One			*Week Two*		
Date	Comment	1–10	Date	Comment	1–10
1.			6.		
2.			7.		
3.			8.		
4.			9.		
5.			10.		

CHAPTER 14

Making the Transition from Living Room to the Public Arena

There are two ways of making the transition from the privacy of your home to the public arena. You can plunge in directly once you have completed the program we have outlined here, or you can go about it more gradually.

First, let us assume you feel ready to confront an actual audience in a public situation. Then we will consider a more gradual transition process.

HOW TO APPROACH YOUR LAUNCHING PAD ON THE DAY OF YOUR BIG TALK

At this point we are assuming that your talk is completely prepared and that you have rehearsed it two times each day for one week (five days).

1. The night before your presentation, pick out exactly what you will be wearing. For women the safest bet is always to wear a suit with an attractive blouse, or a blazer and skirt. Make sure that your outfit is perfectly clean, with no wrinkles. Iron your suit or have it ironed

if you think it will add a look of crispness. A good brushing will always benefit your suit. Be sure that you have your cards numbered and in order.

Both smoking and caffeine affect the sympathetic nervous system, stimulating adrenaline production. Try not to drink any coffee or tea in the twenty-four hours before your talk, if this is at all possible. Or else reduce the amount of caffeine you consume, so as to avoid revving up your bodily processes too much. If you smoke make an effort to cut down on the number of cigarettes you smoke by putting yourself on a cigarette budget the day before your talk.

2. Go to bed at a reasonable time. Do the breathing exercise, counting up to fifty inhalations and exhalations. Doing the breathing exercise will help you fall asleep. If you find that you *cannot* fall asleep, the best thing to do is get up and run through a rehearsal.

3. In the morning, follow your normal routine, but be sure to *give yourself enough time* to do everything, *so that you do not have to rush.* Rushing is disaster to the nervous speaker. Do not drink any coffee or tea; eat lightly and slowly. Do not play loud rhythmic music. Soft relaxing music, however, is always beneficial.

4. Generally try to slow your pace more than usual that day, although I know that this is difficult. When you realize you are moving quickly, try to reduce your speed in *all* activities if possible. Do not walk quickly. Do not get involved in long, complicated discussions, arguments, or —heaven forbid—confrontations. You have too much to lose by allowing your system to become accelerated and stressed. Try to keep an air bubble of space around you. Do some of the body awareness exercises in Chapter 2 at some point in the day.

5. No matter what time your presentation is to occur,

do what good actors do on the day of an important performance:

- Talk less.
- Eat less.
- Don't rush.
- Treat yourself with special love and care.
- Don't go around telling people what is happening to you—be very private.
- Try to follow a simplified mode of behavior.

One of my political clients used to carry on intense conversations up until the very last moment before he would go on an interview talk show. He thought this would give him the sense of being "up" that he felt was so important. He could never understand why on television he came across so hyper and tense.

I never realized what he was doing to himself until one day I accompanied him to a talk show. Although he did his breathing exercises in the car en route to the station, as soon as he got into the studio he became involved in a heated discussion with the other guest on the show.

"Aha!" I said. "The mystery is solved. You say you are following my instructions, but you really are not." Next time I advised no debate until the show was over.

What a difference it made in my client's very next TV appearance. The producer came out after the show to greet him, remarking on how warm and sympathetic his performance had been, especially in light of the controversial subject my client had been discussing. My client was delighted and since that time continues to avoid lengthy discussions before his public appearances.

6. When your time to speak arrives, walk slowly to your meeting room or wherever it is that your talk will take place. If it is in your office, go out and take a short slow

walk in the hall, then return to your office.

7. Once in your meeting room, no matter how much hustle and bustle is going on, try to stay inwardly focused. If you must talk, by all means respond to others, but *keep it short.* Sit in your chair and center yourself immediately. Begin your calm breathing and counting.

When it is your time to speak and your name is called,

- Concentrate on your fingertips.
- Stand up slowly.
- Balance your body.
- Walk slowly and easily to the front of the room, concentrating on your fingertips.
- Turn slowly to face your audience.
- Balance your body again.
- Do a two-second body check.
- Get set by picturing the image or scene where you wish to begin your talk . . . and begin to talk.

INSTRUCTIONS FOR A MORE GRADUAL TRANSITION

Although many prove willing and able to begin testing their skills in a public forum within a matter of weeks, many others find it difficult to make this transition so quickly. This section is designed to guide you through the transition by means of a gradual public rehearsal procedure.

What you need to do is to conduct a test run in front of a small audience, selected by yourself. I would suggest that for your very first venture, you need only one or two people to create the audience-speaker relationship necessary to try out your brand-new presentational skills.

You will need to recruit a friend, coworker, spouse, or other relative for this run-through. Once you have decided on your preview audience, make a definite appointment for a specific time and place. The more formal you are about this, the better it will be for you.

Sit down and work out a complete seven-minute talk, using the Talk-Power model. Be sure to choose a topic that will be of interest to your audience and on which you are well informed. A how-to topic provides an excellent first-run subject.

Remember, you will be inviting your audience to ask formal questions during the question and answer period after your talk. Be prepared first to repeat the question, then to respond briefly but unhurriedly. Be sure also to stick to your time control by using the word budget allowance for a seven-minute talk. Count your words in each section, and cut if you are seriously over your allowance.

When the day of your run-through arrives, try to take it as seriously as you might a real presentation. This means keeping a slow pace as much as possible for the day, eating lightly, not drinking any beverages that contain caffeine, and dressing as if you were really going to be seen by the most important people you know.

This approach will give you an excellent introduction to the preparation necessary for a "real" presentation, and it will help you to feel as good about yourself as possible.

Try to rehearse your talk at least once each day for five days before your run-through, including the day of your presentation. Dress as you would for the real thing.

How Will Your Audience Respond?

Let us assume that you have already done your talk for your first audience. *Do not* ask your audience how they liked your talk. Any "How am I doing?" questions are to be avoided. Here, however, are two questions that you may ask if you wish to benefit from constructive feedback:

1. *Was I clear—did you understand what I was talking about?*
2. *Were you comfortable listening to me—was I too fast or did I show any annoying mannerisms?*

These are the two main areas of concern about your performance that should be of any interest to you in terms of your growth and further development. Concentrate on these two areas. It often happens that any other comments made by your audience may be critical or negative at the expense of your confidence. Suggestions about what you might have said, what the real priorities of the issues are, or complaints that you didn't convince them your point of view was correct are irrelevant.

If you were clear and your audience felt comfortable listening to you, then you are truly on target and ready to do a serious "real world" presentation. If, on the other hand, your audience reports that you were not clear, try to find out what the problem was. Examine the structure of your talk; check your thesis, look at your points. See if your thesis appears in each one of your points, and see what you could have done to clarify your talk.

If your listeners report that they were not comfortable—because you rushed or used nervous gestures or otherwise distracted them with annoying mannerisms—take such feedback seriously, and work on correcting the problems over the next few days of your practice. Then set up another trial run for a second presentation with the same material. Don't bother writing a new one; do the same one until you get it right.

However, if you are left with a discouraged or helpless feeling, it may be wise to invite a different audience for your second open rehearsal. It sometimes happens that a well-meaning friend, spouse, or other person close to you can be overly critical or negative. Their standards may be so impossibly high and unrealistic that you are left with a terrible feeling of inadequacy, even though the same performance might be perfectly acceptable in a professional setting, with your peers and boss as your audience.

If you sense that the reactions you are getting are overly negative, get a second opinion. Even a third or fourth opinion can be helpful, because it gives you the chance to practice in front of a new audience. Use the same talk for each audience. That will give you a clearer view of how you are doing and the progress you are making.

If at the end of these trial runs you still feel unable to get up and make a professional presentation in the "real world," let me recommend a marvelous public speaking organization called Toast-Masters. The Toast-Masters International Speakers Club, with a membership of 100,000, welcomes new members who meet and practice their public speaking skills on a regular basis at meetings, luncheons, and contests, locally, and on a regional basis.

Many graduates of the Talk-Power seminars have joined Toast-Masters to practice and enjoy their newly learned presenting skills.

Expectations

Unrealistic or inappropriate expectations can wreak havoc with the best training programs. Here is a list of constructive, realistic expectations that will help you to cope and grow:

Nervousness
Expect to feel quite nervous. Remember, if you have followed the Talk-Power plan, you will feel nervous, but you will look calm and in-charge.

Confidence
Expect not to feel confident. Confidence comes from an accumulation of successful experiences. You don't necessarily have to feel confident to perform in a poised, confident-looking manner.

Perfection
Expect not to be perfect. You are allowed to come out on top with a much less than perfect performance.

Learning
Expect to learn a great deal about how far along you are in your training program, and also how much more work you must do.

Professionalism
If you follow the program given in this book, you can certainly expect to look and act like a polished professional, no matter how nervous you feel.

Improvement
You can certainly expect to improve your performance with each presentation. Expect this and promise this to yourself.

IN CONCLUSION

I would like to say to you, the reader, just what I say to the students in my seminars: "Yes, there is hope. You can feel good about yourself when you get up to speak." Give yourself that chance. Every minute that you put into working with this program will pay you back a thousand times over. The skills that you will be learning when you do the assignments and rehearsals are permanent lifelong acquisitions.

Just as an actor never forgets or loses his performance skills even if he or she has not performed for many years, once you have trained your mind and body with presentational skills, you will have them for the rest of your life. You will feel good about yourself when you get up to speak. You may always be a little nervous, but you will have the feeling of satisfaction that goes with being able to stand up and express yourself fully and well. If for some reason you stop practicing in the middle of your training period, you can always pick up where you left off, because a skill is a deeply learned experience and becomes a permanent part of who you are and what you can do.

Hava Wolpert Richard, the artist designer, took my seminar in 1977. The next time I saw her was in December 1981, when she delivered an extraordinary speech in honor of her late father, the world-famous silversmith-sculptor Ludwig Y. Wolpert. There were three hundred people present in the auditorium at the Jewish Museum in New York. When the ceremony was over, I watched as Ms. Richard was besieged with guests and friends sharing their feelings of admiration for the beauty and moving simplicity of her presentation. Ms. Richard, a rather shy person, said to me later, "I have not made a speech since I took your course. I worked very hard this week, but it all came back."

I cannot think of anything that compares with the feeling of reward that comes to a teacher when a student shares a moment of professional or personal triumph. Sharing many such moments with hundreds and hundreds of students over the years has given me an enormous feeling of confidence in the reliability and soundness of this program. Not only have I shared moments of triumph, but I have seen the impossible become possible.

Several years ago I had a student who had fainted on the platform during his valedictory address. He went through the program ultimately to become one of the spokespersons for his professional organization. Another young man in one of my classes suffered so severely from the effects of fear of public speaking that he lost his vision whenever he stood in front of an audience. Courage and the positive sense of direction this program was able to provide helped him work his way out of this terrible fear. Today he is a technical consultant for his company and gives lecture demonstrations all over the world.

Not as dramatic but just as satisfying have been the achievements of students who came to the seminars with a minimum of nervousness but whose presentations were quite ordinary and inauspicious. After they had followed through on the rehearsals and assignments, these students sounded like polished speakers, glowing with a wit and charm they had never dreamed they possessed.

These real-life accounts are not unusual. And you are no different from any of these people who began the program with a strong desire to overcome the problems that stood between themselves and speaking in public successfully. You, too, can feel good about yourself when you get up to speak. Give yourself a chance. Keep up with the work. Put aside the small but realistic amount of time that you will need to keep working on the rehearsals and assignments. With only twenty minutes of practice a day for the next three weeks, you can make a major breakthrough in your life.

"Motivation follows action. The more you do, the more you will become motivated to do more." Give yourself a chance.

APPENDIX 1

Panic Clinic for Public Speaking

The Panic Clinic for Public Speaking was designed for people who feel so helpless about speaking in public that they are afraid even to register for a course in public speaking. If you suffer from any of the symptoms listed below, it means that before you will be able to do the regular training exercises given in this book, you will need to practice the special Panic Clinic exercises.

Panic Symptoms

- Rapid heartbeat that is intolerable
- Fear of or actual fainting when speaking before a group
- Hyperventilation (uncontrolled gasping or breathing)
- Feelings of suffocation in front of a group
- Feelings of deep humiliation and shame in front of a group
- Acute disorientation
- Blocking of thought and speech and loss of memory
- Loss of vision or eyes tearing in front of an audience
- Dizziness in front of a group
- Rapid, uncontrolled speaking
- Avoidance of all public speaking situations

The reason individuals suffering from these extreme symptoms need to begin with the Panic Clinic exercises is that the physical distress they are feeling overwhelms their ability to concentrate on feeling particular areas of their body. It is no use telling such people to concentrate on the tingling in their fingertips because, more often than not, they can't even detect that tingling. It is as though these individuals can only experience body signals through extreme panic sensations when they are asked to speak. Only the extreme discomfort of intolerable rapid heartbeat or hyperventilation register as feelings.

The ability to focus attention at will on the various parts of the body is integral to the Talk-Power system. Therefore people with extreme phobias about public speaking must first learn to develop the body awareness skills that are basic to making contact with one's own physical experience in stressful situations.

On the following pages you will find simple exercises to help you to develop an awareness of your inner body experience. Only with such awareness can you learn to control involuntary rapid heartbeat and other physical reactions that accompany a profound phobia about public speaking.

This special program should take you from two to three weeks, working on the exercises for ten or twenty minutes a day. Then you will be able to begin the regular regime for development of speaking abilities.

PANIC CLINIC EXERCISES

Day 1 (10 minutes)

Let us begin with a quiet room—no distractions, no phone calls. Your utmost attention and concentration are necessary. Use a kitchen timer and plan to stop after ten minutes.

You will need an object (a book, an ashtray, a plant) weighing at least two pounds but no more than five pounds.

1. Place the object on a table. Now, from a standing position, pick up the object. Hold the object in your hand and feel the weight of the object as if your hand were a human scale. Do not tighten your muscles around the object; hold it loosely. Do not jiggle; just keep your hand still.

2. Move the object slowly from your right hand to your left hand (count to five). When you move the object from one hand to the other, keep concentrating on the weight in your hand. Do not begin to clutch or tightly hold the object when you change hands with the object. Move it back and forth from the right hand to the left hand five times. Put the object back on the table slowly. Feel the weight until you release it.

3. Sit down and rest. Close your eyes and very slowly count to ten. Try to let go of all tension. Then repeat the above exercise until ten minutes have passed. After this, go about your normal routine. Do not look for results.

Day 2 (10 minutes)

1. Once again in a quiet room, with a kitchen timer set to ten minutes, take out the same object as the day before.

2. Go through the exercise as you did the day before one time. Then sit and rest.

3. After resting for a slow count of ten, pick up the object and walk very slowly with it in your hand to the opposite side of the room. Concentrate on the weight of

the object at all times. Walk slowly. Put the object down. Sit down and rest, closing your eyes and slowly counting to ten.

4. Pick up the object again. Concentrate on its weight. Walk slowly back to your original place, put the object down, and rest, counting to ten with your eyes closed.

Repeat for ten minutes or until kitchen timer rings.

Do not look for results.

Day 3

1. Set up as on days 1 and 2.

You will need the original object plus two others more or less heavy than the original (for example, a one-pound paperweight and a four-pound dictionary in addition to the two-pound plant used before). It is not necessary to weigh the objects, just so long as they have body and feel as if they are of different weights.

2. Pick up each object *slowly,* being aware of the weight, then put it back down. Be aware of the difference in weight of the three objects. Try to keep your body as relaxed as possible while you do this. Be aware of any tensing-up that you do. When you put one object down, try to relax as much as possible before picking up the next one.

3. After you have picked up each object in turn, sit down, close your eyes, and slowly count to ten. Then begin the exercise from the beginning.

Continue until the timer goes off.

Day 4

1. Do the exercise for day 3. Go through the exercise once as you did the day before. . . . Sit and rest.

2. After resting for a slow count of ten, pick up an object and walk across the room with it. Come back and rest, and then pick up the next object and walk across the room. Be sure to rest after every trip. Continue for ten minutes.

Day 5

1. Choose one object weighing two to three pounds.

Choose a nursery rhyme or a favorite song that you know by heart.

2. Stand up and pick up the object, concentrating on the weight as you did on day 1. As you do this, begin reciting the nursery rhyme in a soft whisper. (If you do not feel comfortable with a nursery rhyme, then use a song or any poem that you know well.) Remember not to hold the object tightly, just firmly enough so that you do not drop it.

Hold the object in your hand and stand in place until you have completed the song or rhyme. Be aware of the weight of the object at all times as you recite or sing your song.

3. Sit down and rest. Close your eyes and count to ten. Then repeat the exercise until ten minutes have passed.

Day 6

1. Follow the instructions for day 5, except this time walk across the room holding the object and reciting or singing the song.

2. When you have crossed the room, put down the object, and count to ten. Then pick the object up again, and cross back while reciting or singing your song. Do not rush. Be aware at all times of the weight of the object as

you recite/sing and walk. It is very important that you walk as slowly as possible.

Day 7

1. Stand up.

Working with three objects of different weight, recite/sing while standing in place.

Repeat for ten minutes.

2. Walk across the room with each of your three objects. Be aware of the change in weight with each one. Rest after you cross the room each time.

Repeat for ten minutes.

If you feel ready to go beyond this set of preparatory exercises and begin the Talk-Power system, you will experience

- A general feeling of calm
- A slowing down of your heartbeat
- A slight awareness of body weight or heaviness when you walk
- An easing up of the physical discomfort you previously experienced
- An inhibition of your impulse to move quickly

If you do not feel sufficiently grounded yet, by all means repeat the week's series of exercises again. It is rare that people do not respond to these exercises by the end of three weeks.

Panic Clinic Schedule

Day	Attitude	Time—Start/Finish	Comments	Self-Rating: Calm–Nervous (1–10)
Example	Skeptical	7:30/7:50	Very difficult	7
1				
2				
3				
4				
5				
6				
7				

APPENDIX 2

Advanced Sense-Memory Imaging Rehearsal

Imaging is simply imagining an entire scene in as much detail as possible during a state of deep relaxation. This technique is often used in sports, as mental training for players to handle difficult shots and unexpected events. Players, while in a state of deep relaxation, are taught to imagine the playing of an entire game. Basketball players, skiiers, tennis players, and gymnasts are often tremendously helped by this technique.

Alan Richardson of Australia experimented with three groups of basketball players. After three weeks he concluded that one group that had practiced imaging without engaging in actual physical practice had improved as much as the group that had had physical practice. The third group, which did not practice imaging on the court, showed no improvement.

Combining the acting technique of recalling a sense memory (that is a sensory experience) with imaging, we have what we call Sense-Memory Imaging, imagining a scene with as much sense recall as possible during a state of deep relaxation.

If you would like to add some variety to your rehearsal,

or if you are in a situation where you would like to use your time to rehearse but cannot get up on your feet to speak out loud, Sense-Memory Imaging can be an ideal technique for rehearsing a talk.

Read the instructions carefully before you begin. If you wish, put these instructions on your tape recorder so that you can hear them as you begin relaxing. Be sure that you include a pause wherever you see the dots in the text.

1. Begin to imagine that you are in the room where you are to give your talk. In your imagination, try really to see

The shape of the room . . .

The color of the wall . . .

The light in the room . . .

The furniture. . . . Are there chairs? . . . What color are they? . . .

The other people in the room . . .

What they are wearing . . . (Take your time to look at each person.)

If you feel your level of excitement beginning to rise, that's all right. Just keep breathing, gently inhaling and exhaling.

2. Now imagine yourself sitting in that room. . . . Look at what you are wearing. . . . Look at your shoes or boots . . .

With your fingertips, try in your imagination to feel the fabric of your clothes . . .

Try to hear whatever sounds are in the room . . .

If there are any aromas in that room, try to capture them in your imagination . . .

If by now you are becoming a bit nervous, this is usual.

3. Begin concentrating on the pulse in your fingertips, just as you would for a real presentation. Now that you have imagined the surroundings for your talk, try to

imagine getting up from your seat . . . grounding yourself . . . and then slowly, comfortably walking to the front of your audience.

If your nervousness becomes too acute just begin your calm breathing again and wait until you feel ready to proceed.

4. Begin going through your entire speech. Start with your opening remark and in your imagination go right through each section. The most important thing about this rehearsal is that you *take all of the time you need to do every part of your speech,* including the pauses and rest periods.

If you are using visuals in your talk, image working slowly and carefully with each visual. Try to get the feel of each object you are holding, to see each chart and picture wherever it is placed. The more accurately you can imagine the rehearsal, the more complete will be the benefits.

From time to time look up and try to imagine seeing your audience looking and listening to you . . . silent . . . approving . . . nodding agreement . . .

5. When you have finished your talk, try to imagine the approval and respect you will see on the faces of your audience. . . . Feel that feeling of success. . . . Bask in the pleasure of your own achievement . . .

As you rehearse in the privacy of your own mind, you are developing coping mechanisms: a sense of experience in speaking in public, practice in pacing yourself, an ability to think in terms of presenting, a feeling of being in control.

6. After your talk, begin to visualize your question and answer period, as previously described in Chapter 11. The imaging exercise can be one of the most powerful tools you have for overcoming fear here, as it provides you with

an exposure experience that entails absolutely no risk on your part.

Studies have shown that constant and repeated exposure is one of the best ways to overcome fear. Even though there is no physical movement in your imaging rehearsal, experiments show that when you imagine doing an activity, small electrical charges are registered in the muscles associated with that activity. As a result, the imaging exercise produces an effect similar to a real practice experience.

Repetition of this imaging rehearsal will certainly make for a smoother, more rehearsed presentation.

APPENDIX 3

The Kinesthetic Rehearsal

I have found over the years that a certain percentage of my students and clients respond quite readily to the Talk-Power exercise system yet still report a feeling of detachment when they get up to do their presentations. Although these people are able to get up and present adequately, there is a lingering feeling of not really being connected to their words. It is as if there was no involvement between the speech and the rest of the body.

My hypothesis is that in these people the normal flow of energy into ideas, speech, and gesture is somehow blocked. As a result the following symptoms are reported:

- "Not really feeling the words coming out of my mouth."
- "Feeling as if the words are stuck in my head."
- "Feeling physically stiff and disconnected. Hearing my words but not feeling they are really mine."

The Kinesthetic Rehearsal (a perfect exercise for this problem) is an old acting exercise that will help free you up so that you can be more in touch with your presenting self and feel less tight and inhibited. However, you should not do this rehearsal until you have gone through the entire Talk-Power training program, as the letting go of control it calls for is harmful for a beginning speaker.

For this exercise you need a setup. Take your cards and tape them to a wall in the room where you are going to rehearse so that you can easily see them in front of you without having to hold them.

Now read these instructions carefully, then begin:

1. Sit in a chair. Let go of your tensions, and center yourself. Inhale through your nose and gently blow out through your mouth twenty breaths.
2. Concentrating on your fingertips, stand up. Balance your body in place, then *slowly* walk to the place where your cards are taped on the wall.
3. Rehearse your speech in mime.

There are no spoken words in the Kinesthetic Rehearsal. The entire rehearsal consists of you using your hands, feet, and facial expressions as vigorously as possible, miming (as in charades) each word in your speech. *Vigorous* means bobbing your head, waving your arms, stamping your feet, grimacing. Try to communicate graphically as possible the meaning of each word in your talk *without* speaking. If you do this correctly, you will feel quite energized and relaxed when you finish the exercise.

If you find this exercise difficult or feel inhibited or embarrassed to do it even in a room alone by yourself, you can be sure that this exercise is one you need in order to overcome physical inhibition. Even though it may be uncomfortable at first, if you do this exercise once each day for two weeks in addition to your regular rehearsal, you will find it much easier to carry out an actual presentation. Students report that there is an increase of 50 percent or more in feelings of physical comfort and connectedness when speaking in public after doing this routine.

Remember, just standing up and moving with feeling is not enough. For the Kinesthetic Rehearsal you must try to inject energy and force into the words and meaning of your talk without saying a word aloud. Being able to communicate strong emotions physically frees the energy you need in order to make the subtlety of your ideas come to life.

The Kinesthetic Rehearsal is *not* to be done by a nervous speaker who has not gone through the entire Talk-Power program for at least fourteen days. The reason for this is simply that the violent gestures and motions called for simply reinforce all of the jerks, tics, and involuntary movements of the nervous, untrained beginner. These must first be brought under control.

APPENDIX 4

Participation in Meetings and Classrooms

Fear of public speaking and its effects can create inhibitions that prevent you from expressing yourself in a variety of situations. Many people who come to my seminars report that they are unable to ask questions or make comments in a class. Meetings and conferences are also a problem for the person who has difficulty speaking in public. When the training program is carefully followed, students report that their fears inhibiting participation in classes as well as in conferences have been greatly diminished. However, if you wish to improve your classroom or conference participation even more, you should practice the rehearsal exercise described below. I would like to note here that this exercise has more chance of helping you *after* you have already worked with the basic presentational skills contained in the beginning of the book.

For this exercise you will need to bring your tape recorder to your class or meeting so that, if it is permitted, you can make a tape of the session. If you are not allowed to use a tape recorder in a class, read your class notes onto a tape. The tape should be thirty minutes long.

Step 1

At home when you are ready for your rehearsal, place your tape recorder with the tape you made previously of your class or meeting session near you so that you can turn it off and on easily. Now sit in a chair . . . let go of your tensions . . . center yourself . . . inhale with your nose and exhale with your mouth for twenty breaths. You may keep your eyes open or closed as you wish. Now switch on your tape machine and play the tape of your meeting or class. You will probably feel a jump in your level of tension as soon as you begin to hear the discussion. This is perfectly natural. Just sit listening and breathing. When you feel that you are listening and breathing in a comfortable rhythm, begin to concentrate on your fingertips, listening to the entire tape until it is finished. Rewind your tape.

Step 2

Now write three different questions and three different comments that you might have made had this been a real session. A very good formula for structuring a comment is to say:

In reference to . . .
(or about) . . .
I think that . . .
Because ____________(first reason)____________
and ____________(second reason, if there is one)____________

Example:
In reference to speaking up at meetings, I think that it is very helpful to promise yourself that you will make at least one statement at each meeting that you attend.

Because this systematic plan will quickly reduce your inhibitions about speaking up at meetings, *and* if you make up your mind to do it, you will not have to make a decision about it at the meeting. You will just do it because you have to.

Step 3

Now that you have written out three questions and three comments that are relevant to the discussion on your tape, once again sit in your chair . . . center yourself . . . let go of your tensions . . . inhale with your nose and exhale with your mouth for twenty inhalations and exhalations. Switch on your tape recorder. Sit listening and breathing. When you feel that you are listening and breathing in a comfortable rhythm, concentrate on your fingertips. Now shut off your tape recorder, and if you are going to ask a question say out loud, "I have a question to ask." Then ask your question. If you were going to make a comment say, "I have a comment to make" and give one of the prepared comments that you have just written down. You may read the question or comment if you wish, but speak slowly and clearly.

Step 4

When you have finished your question or comment, turn on the tape recorder and continue listening to your tape. It makes no difference at which point you shut off or turn on your tape recorder and speak. The purpose of this exercise is simply to let you become familiar with the procedure of asking questions and making comments within the context of a classroom or meeting situation.

As you listen to your tape recorder, breathe as before, concentrating on your fingertips. After about five minutes, shut off your tape machine and this time ask another question or make a comment, speaking slowly and clearly. When your question is finished, once again turn on your tape recorder and listen to your tape breathing, concentrating on your fingertips for five minutes more. Then shut off your tape again and keep repeating this procedure until all of your questions and comments have been expressed.

Practice this entire exercise once each day for one week.

After a week of this rehearsal at home, it will be time for you to put yourself on a real life practice schedule. This means that you must decide to ask one question or make one comment at every single class, conference session, or meeting that you attend in the next two weeks. Ask a question even if you know the answer. The point is to speak up once at every single meeting.

If you feel that you are not able or ready to ask questions after one week, then by all means continue rehearsing at home with your tape recorder for one or even two more weeks. However, after the third week you should try a real life experience. If you have done the original training as outlined in the beginning of this book, plus the three weeks of rehearsal at home, you will find that you will probably be able to handle the asking of one simple question or the making of one simple comment in a real situation. Now that you have asked one question at each meeting or classroom session for two weeks, you are ready to make your comments. For the next two weeks decide to ask one question and to make one comment at every single meeting or classroom session that you attend.

Finally, make it a rule, whenever possible, to ask at least one question and make at least one comment at every meeting you attend.

Progress Report for Questions

Week One			*Week Two*		
Date	Comment	Calm–Nervous 1–10	Date	Comment	Calm–Nervous 1–10
1.			6.		
2.			7.		
3.			8.		
4.			9.		
5.			10.		

Part 2—Rehearsal Schedule (Saturday–Sunday optional)

Day	Time Start–Finish	Weak Spot	Strong Spot	Comment	Self-Rating—calm–nervous 1–10
Example	8:30/8:50	2nd point	Introduction–Point section	Need to pause after thesis	6
1					
2					
3					
4					
5					
6					
7					

APPENDIX 5

Video as a Training Tool

In the past several years video as a training tool has gained increasing popularity with speech coaches and in communication programs. For the experienced speaker who has mastered the basic presentational skills, video can be an informative tool for subtle corrective work.

I do *not* recommend video recording as a training tool for beginning or fearful speakers.

When the beginning student's attention is directed to how he looks, whether this is positive or negative, this focus detracts from the effective thrust of the initial steps in the training program. These initial steps concentrate on teaching the student to be aware and to tolerate whatever sensations his or her body is *feeling* in connection with speaking in public. The first step is to direct the student *away* from the external, or visual, perception of his image. The student must learn before all else to concentrate upon the internal experience through *body awareness.* The ability to sustain at will an inner focus or attention has to be mastered first in order for the student to overcome inhibitory blocks and develop presenting skills.

For the inexperienced or fearful speaker, skills of physical control and coordination are as important to progress as they are to the beginning driver. The various skills of response and instant decision-making cannot be learned by watching yourself on a screen. They must initially be experienced in a *feeling* mode. One does not use video to teach people to drive, and it follows that the same rule should apply to beginning or fearful speakers.

APPENDIX 6

Stuttering

From time to time persons who have been stutterers come to my seminars. Some of these people have been in treatment with specialists; others only have a stuttering problem when they try to speak in front of a group. The range of dysfunction varies from slight to a most pronounced impairment of speech.

These students are integrated into the regular program and do exactly the same exercises as the other students. The only modification in their training is that when they begin to stutter during their talk, I place a lightly weighted object (a salt shaker) in each hand and ask the student to concentrate on the weight of the object as he or she speaks before the group. In each case, the stuttering stops as if by a miracle. The effect is so obvious and immediate that at times there are gasps in the class at the clear speech of a previously stuttering student now unwaveringly completing his or her speech.

In more advanced portions of the program, these same students no longer hold the weighted objects, but are told to imagine that they are still holding the shakers. This has to be done very carefully, because if one only pretends to hold the object without really imaging it, the exercise will not work. However, with the correct imaging procedure—really sending attention into the fingertips and hands so that one genuinely imagines the "feel" of the weights—the stuttering student can maintain the clarity of speech achieved before with the actual weights.

I advise people wanting to try this exercise to use light weighted objects such as a key ring or a small rock, weighing from a few ounces to one pound at the most. Two to four weeks should be spent working with the actual weights before one tries imaging the weights in each hand. This is because one must learn the feel of these objects before it is possible to begin successfully imaging them.

Index

Action Formula Word Budget, 77, 78, 80
Acting training and technique, 1, 2; and public speaking, 2, 3, 27, 178
Anxiety, 97; anticipatory, 195. *See also* Distress; Fear response; Public speaking, fear response and nervousness
Assertiveness, lack of, 183-92; and women, 189-92
Assertiveness Test, 184
Attention skills (speaker's), 19
Audience: constructive feedback, 208; debating within question and answer period, 169; directing attention of, 71, 87, 92, 97, 98; distracting, 54; last chance to get through to, 137; making good impression on, 77; motivating, 81, 82, 108-20; response, 207-213
Autonomic nervous system, 58

Balance awareness, 35, 38, 58
Baruch College, 2
Baryshnikov, 21
Behavior modification, 3, 26, 53, 183
Bobbing head habit, 48, 57; exercise for, 57-58
Body awareness, 20, 58
Body movements, 56
Book of Lists, 8
Borman, Frank, 100
Brain: left and right sides, 27-29; "old mammalian," 23; physiology of, 23-26; "reptilian," 23, 25
Brainstorming, 124-26
Breathing, 48, 58-59, 61-62; exercises for, 59-60, 204
Brevity, 116. *See also* Speech(es), length and individual sections
The Building-Block Approach, 70-80

Caffeine, 204
Centering, 58, 60
Cerebral cortex (neocortex), 23-24
Charisma, 19
"Chunking," 126-27
Clothing (for public speaking), 203
Complete speech, preparing, 148-55
Concentration, 19, 33
Confidence, lack of, 186, 188
Connecting a point to your thesis, 130-33
Conversation (as opposed to public speaking), 13, 17; feedback in, 13, 14; "rules" in, 14, 41
Conversational skills, 17
Coordination skills, 19
Corporate speaking, 7-8, 16-17, 100-101, 108-109, 110, 113, 114-16, 191
Criticism, 86

Demonstration talk, 161-67
Distress: learning to control, 18, 25;

Distress *(cont.)*
mental, 10-11, 38, 40; physical, 9-11, 16, 17, 21, 24, 30-31, 38, 40, 55, 186. *See also* Anxiety; Fear response; Public speaking, fear response and nervousness
Dowling, Colette, 189
Drifting during talk, 123

East-West Method, 86
Electronic aids, 58-60; preparation, 60; purpose of, 59
Emotional awareness, 38, 40
Emotional control, 8, 19
Emotional reactions, 10-11
Expectations, unrealistic, 209
Expressive gestures, 55, 56
Eye contact, 40-42

Facing the audience, 37-39
Fear response: causes of, 7-29; controlling, 5, 6, 8, 30-42. *See also* Anxiety; Distress; Public speaking, fear response and nervousness
Feedback, 13, 208
Fensterheim, Dr. Herbert, 61
File cards, 104, 106, 117, 119; limited space on, 117
Films, 58

Goal clarification, 127

Heartbeat, rapid, 18, 21, 31, 35, 48, 214. *See also* Distress, physical
Humanizing yourself, 110-111
Hyperventilation, 61-62, 214. *See also* Breathing

IBM, 2
Imagination, 20
Imaging. *See* Sense-Memory Imaging; Visualization
Inability to speak, 9
Involuntary movement, 55

Jensen, David, 59
Jewish Museum, 211

Kinesthetic Rehearsal, 225-27

LaGuardia Community College, 2
"Launching pad," 30; and control, 31
Lennenberg, Eric, 72
Lloyd, Chris Evert, 21

May, Rollo, 16
Memory, 126; loss, 48, 49, 211
Mental blocking, 40
Method school of acting, 27
Moskowitz, Breyne Arlene, 14
Moving hands, 48

National Congress for Neighborhood Women, 2
92nd Street YM/YWHA, 2
Nonverbal fillers, 48, 52, 53

Panic Clinic for Public Speaking, 5, 28-29, 214-20
Panic symptoms, 214. *See also* Distress; Fear response
Parasympathetic nervous system, 59
Pausing to gain control, 48
Penney, J.C., 2
Perdue, Frank, 100
Personal history: appropriate, 110-11; inappropriate, 113
Phrases, direct, 99
Present Time Exercise, 27, 38-40
Present Time Inventory, 39
Presentational self, 13
Presentational techniques, 13
Psychological distance, 49
Public Speaker's Bill of Rights, 187, 191, 192
Public speaking: avoiding, 16, 121; building-block approach, 4-6; effective versus ineffective, 70; exercises for, 31, 33, 34, 35, 36, 39, 45, 48, 49, 51, 52, 54, 57, 58, 81, 82, 89, 94, 104, 105, 119, 126, 130, 133, 135, 138, 139, 145, 147, 148, 165, 173, 179, 192, 214-20, 221-24, 225-27, 229-31; fear response and, 3, 5, 6, 8, 16, 30-42, 60, 228 *(see also* Anxiety; Distress;

Fear response); formal response and, 13; goals in, 146-47; intention, 81, 83; jokes in, 43, 44, 46, 50, 62-69, 84-85; lack of training, 16, 186; losing control during, 37, 48; memory and, 46 (*see also* Memory); natural ability and, 8; nervousness and, 1, 11, 30, 116-17 (*see also* Anxiety; Distress; Fear response); pausing during, 48; performance skills and, 17, 18; presentational techniques and, 13; professional, 9; traditional techniques, ineffectuality of, 3, 4, 73-74

Questions from the floor: abusive, 177-78; answering, 168-82; confrontational, 169; fear of, 168; length of answer, 169; limiting, 169; listing possible, 173-76; long, 172; potentially embarrassing, 175; preparation for, 173-77; purpose, 168; repeating, 170; unanswerable, 171
Quotations, use of, 87-89

Rehearsal for speeches, scheduling time for, 199-201
Relating to the audience, 110-111. *See also* Audience
Relaxation, 20-21; misconceptions regarding, 21
Research for speeches, 194; scheduling time for, 194-95
Resistance skills, 20
Rhetorical questions, 87
Richard, Hava Wolpert, 211
Richardson, Alan, 221
Russell, Peter, 126

Self-control, 19
Self-defeating attitudes, 186
Self-defeating mechanisms, 9
Self-editing, 116-19
Sense-Memory Exercise, 27
Sense-Memory Imaging, 221-24; rehearsal, 178, 179-82. *See also* Visualization
Sentence structure, 72
Shocking statements (to gain audience attention), 87
Sitting (on platform), 31-32
Sleep (night before speaking), 204
Slides, 158
Slowing down, 31
Smoking, 204
Social self, 13
Speaking: average speed, 76, 118; fast, 43, 48, 51; how to begin, 43; inaudible, 43; manner of, 43; and stuttering, 236-37
Speech(es): background, 72, 75, 76, 77, 108-120; beginning, 104-105; building excitement in, 134; choosing a topic for, 80-90; climax, 72, 75, 77, 137-39; conclusion, 141-55; corporate, 7-8, 16-17, 100-101, 108-9, 110, 113, 114-16, 191; developing ideas in, 122; ineffective, 1, 70; intention in, 146-47; introductory paragraph, 72, 75, 76, 77; jokes in, 43, 44, 46, 50, 84-85; length, 28, 75, 76-79, 193; organizing, 5, 71, 122; physical preparation for, 106-7; point section, 121-40; practicing, 105-6, 119-20; professional sounding, 119, 210; reading, 118; research for, 193, 194; seven basic sections, 4-5 (*see also* individual sections); structure, 72, 73 (*see also* individual sections); thesis message, 129-30, 131, 133, 138; thesis sentence, 72, 75, 77, 84, 86, 97-98, 100, 101-3; topic sentence, 72, 75, 77, 79, 84, 87, 92-96, 104, 111, 123, 124, 126; when to begin, 37, 40, 42, 43. *See also* Public speaking; Speaker; Speechwriting
Speechwriting, 3, 4, 5, 80-90, 95; craft, 28, 183. *See also* Speech(es)
Speaker: commitment, 98; enthusiasm, 98; inexperienced, 43, 51, 52, 54, 86, 234; lack of assertiveness, 183-92; point of view, 98; relation to audience, 3, 5, 49 (*see also* Audience); role of, 13
Standing (to speak), 34

Stanislavsky, 27
Stuttering, 236-37
Sympathetic nervous system, 58-59

Talk-Power, 2, 3; Action Formula, 28, 70-80; Game Plan, 196-97; Production schedule, 193; System, 3, 4, 5, 58, 81, 122; for Women, 189-92
Tape recorder, 180, 228
Tapes, 158
Technical material, explaining, 161
Telling a story, 43, 44, 46, 50; rehearsal for, 45
Texas A&M University, 84
"Thinking on your feet," 20
Toast-Masters International Speakers Club, 209
Tolstoy, Leo, 70
Training to slow down, 31, 34
Transitions, 74

Vidal, Gore, 173
Video, 234-35
Visual aids, 156-57; chart as, 157; choosing, 156; poster as, 157; purpose of, 156
Visualization, 20, 50-51, 147, 179-80, 221-24
Vocal skills, 20

Warmth, 19
Wolpert, Ludwig Y., 211
Women and public speaking, 189-92
Word budget, 76